FACT
FINDER

NIGHT
SKY

FACT
FINDER

NIGHT
SKY

B R I A N · J O N E S

CRESCENT BOOKS
New York

A SALAMANDER BOOK

First published by Salamander Books Ltd,
129–137 York Way,
London N7 9LG,
United Kingdom.

This 1990 edition published by Crescent Books,
distributed by Crown Publishers Inc.,
225 Park Avenue South,
New York, New York 10003.

ISBN 0 517 03395 X

hgfedcba

CREDITS

Editor: Roseanne Eckart
Designer: Roger Hyde
Captions: Carole Stott
Artwork: © Salamander Books Ltd, except pages 16 and 26
© Starland Picture Library

Printed and bound in Belgium

THE AUTHOR

Brian Jones is an astronomy and spaceflight writer-broadcaster.
He has written three previous books and contributed to a number
of others for children and adults. He writes numerous articles on
astronomy and appears regularly on television and radio.
This book is dedicated by him: To Mum and Dad.

CONTENTS

THE MOVING EARTH

A 'day' is the word generally used to describe the time it takes for the Earth to rotate on its axis. The rotation of the Earth causes night and day. Daytime occurs for the side of the Earth facing the Sun, and night takes place when that side is facing away from our star. The rotation of the Earth also causes the stars and other objects in the sky to appear to rise and set — this apparent motion is always in the direction from east to west across the sky.

Solar and sidereal days

The true rotational period of the Earth is 23hr 56min 4·09sec. This period is called a *sidereal* day (from the Latin word *sidus* meaning *star*) and is equal to the period between successive passages across the meridian of a star. The meridian is an imaginary line reaching from the north point on the horizon, through the overhead point and down to the south point on the horizon. The meridian is not fixed but refers to the sky that an observer sees from anywhere on the Earth's surface. In other words, if a star is due south (on the meridian) at midnight on a particular night, it will reach the same position just under four minutes sooner the following night.

A *solar* day (from the Latin *sol* meaning *Sun*) is 24 hours long and is the interval between successive meridian passages of the Sun. Another way of saying this is that it is the time between successive noons. However, the solar day is a little longer than the sidereal day. This is because the Earth is orbiting the Sun, and we see the Sun from a slightly different position from day to day. In other words, it is like viewing a tree (the Sun) from a moving car (the Earth). The tree will appear to move against the background although it is actually the car that is moving.

During the course of one orbit around the Sun (a year), our star will appear to travel completely round the sky. The apparent motion of the Sun is in an easterly direction. As a result, the solar day is slightly longer than the sidereal day because the Sun has to 'catch up' each time.

The Zodiac

The imaginary sphere which completely surrounds the Earth is known as the *celestial sphere*. The stars and other celestial objects are seen against its surface. The apparent motion of the Sun through the sky means that we see it superimposed against a different area of the celestial sphere from day to day. Its apparent course around the sky appears to take it from west to east through a band of constellations. We call this band the *Zodiac*, and the actual path of the Sun through the Zodiac is called the *ecliptic*.

The seasons

It is the tilt of the Earth's axis relative to the plane of its orbit around the Sun that gives rise to the seasons, rather than the variations in the distance of the Earth from the Sun. In June the northern hemisphere is tilted *towards* the Sun. As a result, the Sun will appear to be *higher* in the sky when seen from locations in the northern hemisphere. This corresponds to the northern *summer* when the days are longer and warmer. Because the southern hemisphere is tilted *away* from the Sun at this time, the southern *winter* will take place. The situation is reversed six months later. In December, the northern hemisphere is tilted *away* from the Sun, and the southern hemisphere *towards* it, thus producing northern *winter* and southern *summer*.

Below: *The Earth's axis is tilted away from the vertical of its orbital plane by some 23.5°. In June, the sun thus shines more directly on the northern hemisphere, causing summer conditions.*

The glancing sunlight on the southern hemisphere gives less intense heat. Six months later, the position is reversed. The Earth is closest to the Sun, and moves fastest in January.

As well as creating the seasons, the tilt of the Earth's axis affects the apparent motion of the Sun through the sky. In northern summer, the Sun appears to be higher in the sky than in northern winter. In other words, during the course of a year, the Sun appears to travel not only from west to east (due to the motion of the Earth around the Sun) through the sky, but also alternatively northwards and southwards (due to the alternate tilt of the Earth's axis towards and away from the Sun). As a result, when the ecliptic is projected against a chart of the zodiacal region of the sky, it resembles a wave form.

The solstices and equinoxes

On or around 21st June and 22nd December, the Earth's axis is tilted directly towards the Sun; the northern hemisphere in June and the southern hemisphere in December (see diagram on The Seasons). At noon on these dates the Sun will reach its highest positions in the sky for those observers in the hemisphere tilted towards the Sun, and its lowest for those in the hemisphere tilted away. The highest and lowest positions of the Sun are known as the *solstices* and correspond to the 'crests' of the wave-like apparent journey of the Sun through the sky. Midsummer Day (longest day and shortest night) and Midwinter Day (shortest day and longest night) occur at these times.

The tilt of the Earth's axis relative to the plane of its orbit around the Sun is 23·5°. Therefore, the maximum tilt of the Earth towards or away from the Sun is 23·5°. The highest and lowest latitudes from which the Sun can ever be seen directly overhead are 23·5°N (the Tropic of Cancer) or 23·5°S (the

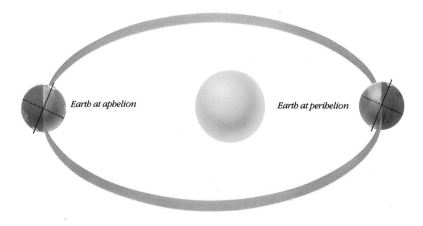

Earth at aphelion   Earth at perihelion

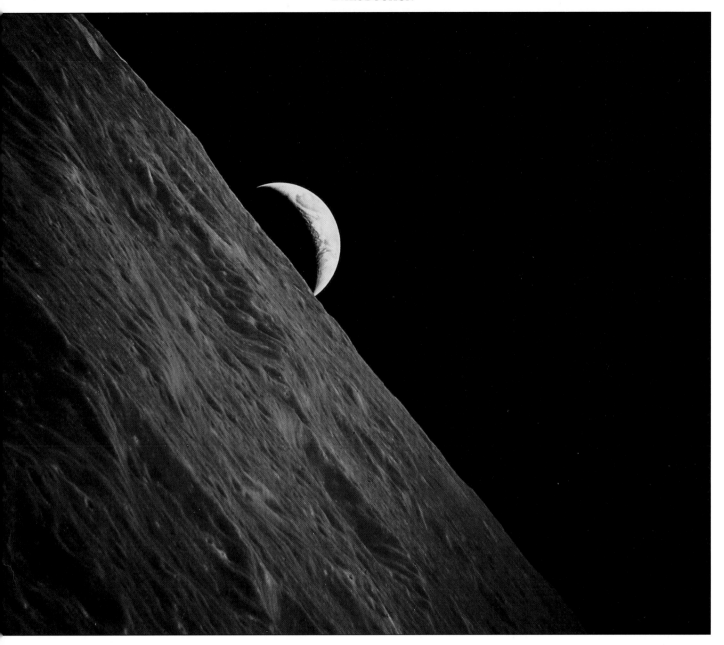

Above: *Earthrise seen from the Moon. The Sun shines on the Earth's disc to form a crescent.*

Tropic of Capricorn). At the solstices the Sun passes overhead at these latitudes, at 23·5°N in June and 23·5°S in December.

The *equinoxes* are the points at which the ecliptic crosses the celestial equator (see page 9). The vernal equinox is crossed as the Sun moves from south to north, and the autumnal equinox as it moves back towards the south. When the Sun is at either of the equinoxes, day and night are the same length.

The durations of the longest day and shortest night depend upon the latitude of the observer. The greater the distance from the equator, the greater the differences. From the equatorial regions (between the Tropics of Cancer and Capricorn), the hours of day and night are of similar lengths. From London the longest day is around 16 hours duration and the shortest around eight hours. From within 23·5° of the Poles (the Arctic and Antarctic Circles), the longest amount of continuous daylight is 24 hours — and there is a midnight Sun in mid-summer. At the North and South Poles day and night are each of six months duration.

THE CELESTIAL SPHERE

As we have seen, the celestial sphere is the imaginary sphere of sky that completely surrounds the Earth. The stars are considered to be fixed on the celestial sphere while the apparent motion of the Sun and the actual orbits of the planets result in their motions against the background of stars.

The celestial poles and celestial equator

The rotation of the Earth actually makes it seem as if the celestial sphere rotates around the Earth. This apparent rotation is centred on the Earth and takes place on an axis joining the *north* and *south celestial poles*. These are two points on the celestial sphere which lie directly above the north and south terrestrial poles. They can be taken to be the points on the celestial sphere through which projections of the Earth's axis would intersect the celestial sphere.

The north celestial pole (NCP) is marked (or almost so!) by the star Polaris in Ursa Minor (see chart on page 54). The nearest star to the south celestial pole (SCP) is the faint Sigma Octantis. As the Earth rotates, the stars on the celestial equator appear to revolve around these two stars. Just as the celestial poles are projections of the Earth's axis of rotation, the celestial equator is a projection of the Earth's equator onto the sky. The celestial equator lies at an angular distance of 90° from *both* celestial poles.

Altitude of the poles

The altitude (angular distance) of the NCP above the northern horizon (or the SCP above the southern horizon) is equal to the latitude of the observer. For example, if you were stood at the north pole (latitude 90°N), the altitude of the NCP would be 90°. In other words, it would be at the zenith. The zenith is the point in the sky that is directly above the observer. This is not a fixed point, but refers to the point in the sky above *wherever* the observer is stood on the Earth's surface.

The further away you are from the north pole, the lower the NCP will be in the sky. From Paris (latitude 49°N) it will have an altitude of 49°, and from the equator (latitude 0°), it will have an altitude of 0°. From the equator Polaris will be seen on the northern horizon, and from below the equator it will be hidden by the Earth and not seen at all.

The same is true for Sigma Octantis — the star marking the SCP — as seen from the

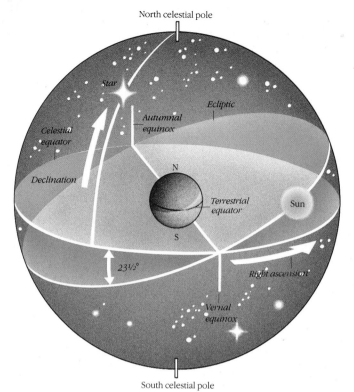

North celestial pole

Star

Autumnal equinox

Ecliptic

Celestial equator

Declination

N

Terrestrial equator

Sun

S

23½°

Right ascension

Vernal equinox

South celestial pole

Left: Celestial co-ordinates from which the positions of celestial objects can be specified precisely on the celestial sphere.

Below: Observers in the northern hemisphere see that the stars appear to rotate about Polaris, the Pole Star. This bright star marks the north celestial pole. This is because it lies above the northerly end of Earth's axis. But the Earth's axis has not always pointed at Polaris. It describes a small circle in the sky over a period of 25,800 years. During this period other stars can lie above the North Pole. This effect is called precession. The small secondary 'wobble' shown, nutation, is an added effect of the Moon's gravity on the Earth.

southern hemisphere. From the south pole it will be overhead, while from the equator it will be seen to skim the southern horizon. From Melbourne (latitude 38°S) it will be 38° above the southern horizon. The celestial poles lie at compass points north and south. In other words, you would be looking due north if gazing at Polaris and due south if gazing at Sigma Octantis.

It is not only Polaris that would be hidden from view to an observer south of the equator. Stars near the NCP would also be hidden — more and more stars are hidden from sight the further south you go. The same is true for observers north of the equator. The further north you travel, the more stars disappear below the southern horizon. Consequently, from any latitude north (or south) of the equator, there are stars permanently hidden around the SCP (or NCP). From the north pole (or south pole), only those stars north (or south) of the celestial equator will ever be seen. For example, the well-known group of stars we call the Plough lie so close to the NCP that they are never seen by observers in the Falkland Islands. The southern constellation Crux is hidden to observers in Great Britain.

Precession

The position of the NCP (and SCP) are slowly changing. This is because of a 'wobble' in the Earth's axis of rotation. This wobble, which is similar to that of a spinning top slowing down, is called precession and is caused by the gravitational influences of the Sun and Moon on the Earth's equatorial bulge. Each wobble takes 25,800 years, during which time the celestial poles trace out circles on the celestial sphere. The change in position of the NCP in relation to the stars is shown here. The SCP traces out a similar circle among the stars in the region of the SCP. The radii of the circles traced out by the celestial poles is 23·5°, which is the angular tilt of the Earth's axis relative to the plane of its orbit around the Sun.

At present Polaris lies very close to the NCP, although this has not always been the case. Because of precession, the star Thuban in the constellation Draco marked the position of the NCP around 4,500 years ago. Eventually, some 12,000 years from now, the brilliant star Vega in Lyra will mark this position.

Left: *In this southern-sky photograph the camera shutter has been left open for several hours. The movement of the stars has been caught on film. The stars rotate about the south celestial pole and produce trails of light. The dome houses the 150in (381cm) Anglo-Australian telescope at Siding Spring, Australia. The astronomer's moving lights have also been caught by the camera.*

Precession of the equinoxes

In the same way that the celestial poles move, the celestial equator moves around the ecliptic. Therefore, the two points at which the celestial equator crosses the ecliptic (the equinoxes) travel along the ecliptic, taking 25,800 years to move completely around the sky. The position of the vernal equinox (also known as the First Point of Aries) is constantly changing. Although around 2,000 years ago it lay in the constellation of Aries (hence the alternative name), it has since moved into Pisces and will enter Aquarius a few centuries from now. The present period preceding its entry into Aquarius has given rise to the phrase 'dawning of the age of Aquarius' — so dear to our astrological friends!

THE FORMATION OF THE SOLAR SYSTEM

The planets are split into two distinct groups. Mercury, Venus, Earth and Mars are the terrestrial planets (from the Latin word *terra* meaning *earth*). These are all small, rocky worlds. Jupiter, Saturn, Uranus and Neptune are the gas giants. They are all large and gaseous in composition.

Birth of the planets

The Solar System was formed from the solar nebula — a rotating cloud of gas, dust particles and ice. The rotation of the solar nebula caused it to form a disc, with the Sun in the central region (see Stellar Evolution), and the material in the surrounding disc forming the planets. The terrestrial planets were composed of the heavier elements in the central regions, the gaseous planets forming mainly from hydrogen, helium and other lighter elements nearer the outer edges of the cloud.

Particles within the inner regions collided with each other and stuck together, accumulating into larger and larger objects to form the terrestrial planets. At this stage they consisted of molten rock. The heavier elements sank towards their central regions leaving the lighter, less dense material near their surfaces. This produced the iron-rich cores and rocky outer regions of the terrestrial planets seen today.

The outer planets evolved in a similar way, but the initial rocky objects eventually collected up the gas that abounded in the outer regions of the solar nebula. The end result was huge gaseous planets with rocky cores and atmospheres rich in hydrogen.

The central region of the rotating cloud collapsed to form the Sun, the energy from which swept most of the remaining debris out into space, leaving the Solar System much as it is today. Many of the remaining particles (some of which were quite sizeable) fell onto the newly formed planets, creating the rugged, crater-strewn surfaces that exist today.

The Sun

The light and heat from our parent star makes life on Earth possible. However, the Sun only appears bright and powerful because it is much closer than other stars. It has a diameter of 865,000 miles (1,392,530km) and its closeness gives us the opportunity to observe a typical star.

Visual appearance

The outer visible surface of the Sun is the photosphere — a name which means 'sphere of light'. It temperature is around 11,000°F (6,000°C), and it is from this outer surface that the Sun's light and heat emerges. However, the energy that leaves the Sun is actually created at its core, where the temperature (27 million °F (15 million °C)) and immense pressure (340,000 million times the atmos-

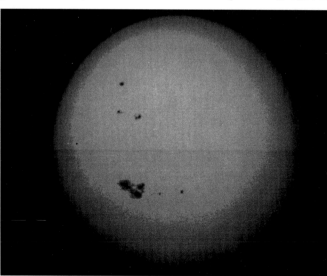

Left: *The Sun is the closest star to us and the only one that we can observe in detail. It is possible to record sunspots; dark patches on the Sun's visible surface.*

Right: *The Sun is a large ball of gas, mainly hydrogen but with a substantial proportion of helium. It is hot and dense at the centre, and cooler and thinner at the surface. Its energy is produced in its core (1) as hydrogen converts to helium. The heat is transferred through its*

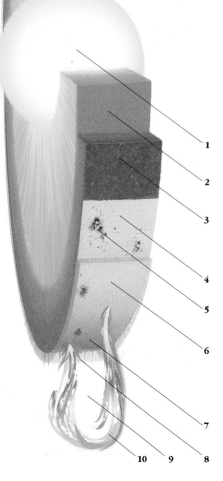

interior (2 and 3) to the visible surface of the Sun, the photosphere (4). This has a granular appearance (7). Sunspots (5) occur on this surface. Above the photosphere is the rarefied atmosphere of the chromosphere (6). Flame-like projections which are hot hydrogen gas (8) surge through it to the Sun's outer atmosphere, the corona (9). Other features are solar flares (10) and prominences.

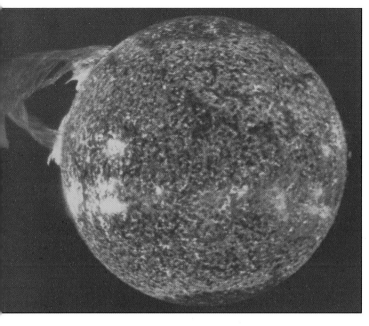

Left: *The space station Skylab orbited Earth for over six years in the 1970's. It took nearly 300,000 pictures of the Sun. This one shows a giant, twisted flame-like cloud in the upper atmosphere of the Sun. It is a prominence - a region of material at a lower temperature but with a higher density than its surroundings. They usually originate in the vicinity of sunspots or other active solar regions and the only time they can be seen in white light is during a total solar eclipse. This view was taken in far ultra violet light.*

do not try this!). A typical sunspot has a dark central region, known as the umbra, where the temperature is around 7,000°F (4,000°C). This is surrounded by a lighter, slightly hotter penumbra. Sunspots can appear at any time, although there is a definite cycle over which sunspot activity reaches a maximum once every 11 years. Faculae are highly luminous clouds of gas, comprising primarily hydrogen and are regions above the photosphere where sunspots are about to form. Other features include prominences — huge columns of gas which appear above sunspots — and flares — bright filaments of hot gas arising in complex sunspot groups.

Above the photosphere lies the chromosphere, through which solar energy passes on its way out from the Sun. Faculae and flares are seen in the chromosphere. The outermost region of the Sun's atmosphere is the corona, which stretches out from just above the chromosphere to a distance of several million miles. Prominences appear within the inner regions of the corona — its outer regions eventually becoming the stream of energised particles called the solar wind.

pheric pressure at the Earth's surface) are such that nuclear reactions take place. This reaction is known as hydrogen burning, and during the process four nuclei of hydrogen are fused together to form one nucleus of helium. There is a tiny amount of mass left over from the reaction which makes its way to the surface from where it escapes as light and heat.

The eruption of energy at the surface gives the photosphere a mottled effect known as granulation. Energy from within the Sun forms bright granules surrounded by darker boundaries. The bright areas are regions where hot gases are emerging, which then cool and spill down through the darker boundaries.

Sunspots are also seen on the photosphere. These are depressions in the solar surface which appear as dark patches against the brighter, hotter background. Sunspots are typically several tens of thousands of miles across, although some spots are so large that they can be seen with the naked eye (however

Observing the Sun

Sunspots are the easiest solar feature to observe. Sunspot numbers vary throughout the solar cycle. At times of minimum activity you may find the Sun totally devoid of spots for several days or even weeks at a time. However, at maximum activity the solar disc may be swarming with spots! If you project the entire solar disc (see diagram of Solar Projection) you can either mark off the positions of sunspots or draw in their outlines. If done on a weekly basis, these observations could eventually build up into a record on sunspot activity — perhaps over a complete solar cycle.

Faculae are seen as bright patches of light against the photosphere. They can be observed near the centre of the disc, although they are more easily seen near the limb (the edge of the visible disc of the Sun). These bright clouds of hydrogen are roughly as bright as the photosphere, and there is little contrast between faculae and the photosphere near the centre of the solar disc. They are much more prominent near the limb because they appear in the chromosphere which is several hundred miles above the photosphere.

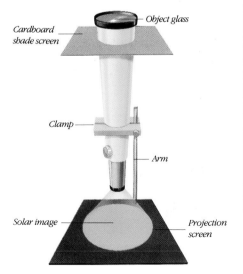

Cardboard shade screen

Object glass

Clamp

Arm

Solar image

Projection screen

The Sun's mass loss

The mass lost by the Sun due to hydrogen burning is equal to less than 1 per cent of the total amount of hydrogen used in the reaction. This does not sound much until you consider the fact that 600 million tons of hydrogen are being converted into helium every second! The total mass loss is about 4 million tons per second! Yet, the Sun has been shining for around 5,000 million years and contains enough material for it to continue to do so for a further 5,000 million years!

The Sun is the brightest and most visually accessible object for astronomers. However, its brightness makes it a potential hazard to observers who do not take precautions. You must never look directly at the Sun, especially not through a telescope or binoculars. Instead, use solar projection (see diagram left).

THE MOON

With a diameter of 2,172 miles (3,476km) the Moon is over a quarter of the size of the Earth. When we look at other planet and satellite systems, we see that the planet is nearly always considerably larger than the satellites which orbit it. There is so little difference between the sizes of Earth and Moon (compared to differences in sizes between other planets and their satellites) that our system can be regarded as a double planet rather than a planet and satellite.

The Moon rotates every 27·3 days — the same length of time that it takes to orbit the Earth. This means that the Moon keeps the same face turned towards the Earth. However, the distance between the Earth and Moon varies from 222,756 miles (356,410km) at its closest to 254,186 miles (406,697km) at its furthest. The Moon's orbital speed alters slightly because of this, and the axial rotation and revolution periods get slightly 'out of step'. This makes the Moon 'wobble' a little. This wobble is known as libration, and it allows the observer to see up to 59 per cent of the lunar surface.

The formation of the Moon

Many different ideas have been put forward to explain the origin of the Moon, the most popular being the Collision Ejection Theory. This states that an object similar in size to Mars collided with the Earth long ago. According to the theory, both the Earth and the smaller object had already formed central metallic cores, surrounded by thick mantles of rock. When the object hit the Earth it disintegrated. Its core stuck to our planet, but the debris that resulted from the collision was ejected into orbit around the Earth and

Illustration of the Moon's near side with labelled features:

SEA OF COLD
PLATO
SEA OF RAINS
ARISTARCHUS
APENNINES
SEA OF SERENITY
COPERNICUS
SEA OF CONFLICTS
OCEAN OF STORMS
SEA OF VAPOURS
SEA OF TRANQUILLITY
SEA OF FERTILITY
SEA OF HUMORS
SEA OF NECTAR
TYCHO
LEIBNITZ MOUNTAINS

Left: *The Moon is the brightest object in the night sky, even though it has no light of its own. It simply reflects sunlight. Some of its features are easy to see without using any optical aid. The dark flat areas of land are maria, from the Latin, mare, for sea. They were given this name because early astronomers thought they were seas. The lighter areas are mountainous land. Binoculars will show some of the craters.*

Right: *Between July 1969 and December 1972 American astronauts spent just less than 80 hours exploring the Moon's surface.*

eventually collected together to form the Moon. Examination of the lunar rocks brought back by the Apollo astronauts has convinced astronomers that this is what happened. The overall density of the Moon is similar to that of the Earth's outer layers. Also, the chemical compositions of the Earth and Moon are very similar.

The lunar surface

Most of the lunar surface comprises bright, heavily cratered highland terrain. These areas contrast with the much darker lunar plains. Long ago, before the invention of the

telescope, it was thought that the dark areas were actually expanses of water. We now know that there is no water on the Moon, although the romantic names given to these areas such as Mare Serenitatis (Sea of Serenity), Palus Nebularum (Marsh of Mists) and Oceanus Procellarum (Ocean of Storms) are still used today.

The lunar plains were formed between 3 and 4 billion years ago as lava welled up from the lunar interior and filled the low lying areas of the lunar surface. By this time, the main period of meteoritic bombardment (see pages 30-31) that had peppered the surfaces of the Moon and other rocky planets, had subsided. The comparative lack of cratering on the maria (large lunar plains) indicates that these areas were formed relatively recently in the Moon's history, after the main period of meteoritic bombardment.

Lunar eclipses

Lunar eclipses occur when the Moon passes into the Earth's shadow. During a lunar eclipse the sunlight, which normally illuminates the Moon, is temporarily cut off, resulting in the Moon being plunged into darkness. The Moon rarely becomes completely invisible as some sunlight is usually bent, or 'refracted', onto the lunar surface by the Earth's atmosphere. Generally speaking, the

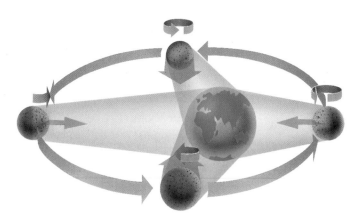

Left: *As the Moon orbits the Earth it rotates on its axis. On each orbit the Moon makes one complete rotation. As a result the same face of the Moon is presented to Earth. However, variations in the Moon's orbital speed cause it to appear to swing slightly from side to side (libration). In fact 59 per cent of the surface is revealed during a full orbit.*

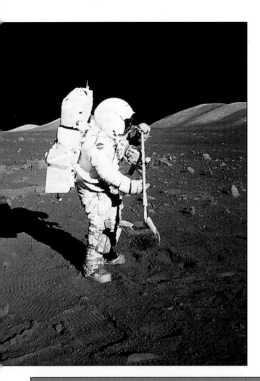

Moon takes on a deep coppery-red colour during a lunar eclipse.

The Earth's shadow has two distinct regions: a dark, central umbra (shadow) and a surrounding area of partial shadow called the penumbra. These different areas of shadow give rise to three types of lunar eclipse. A total lunar eclipse takes place when the Moon passes through the umbra, at which time an observer on the lunar surface would see the Sun pass completely behind the Earth. A partial eclipse takes place when only part of the Moon passes through the umbra. If the Moon passes through the penumbra — a penumbral eclipse takes place. Our observer located on the Moon would see only *part* of the Sun's disc disappear behind the Earth. Penumbral eclipses are very difficult to detect as the darkening effect of the Earth's penumbral shadow is only very slight.

Solar eclipses

Although the Sun is much larger than the Moon, it is also much further away. As a result, both the Sun and Moon appear to be roughly the same size as seen from Earth. Solar eclipses take place when the Moon passes between the Earth and the Sun, at which times all or part of the Sun's light is blotted out.

There are three different types of solar eclipse. Total eclipses occur when the lining up of the Sun, Moon and Earth is exact, and the Moon completely hides the solar disc. Partial eclipses take place when the lining up is not exact and only part of the Sun is hidden. Annular eclipses also occur when the lining up is exact, but when the Moon is at or near its furthest point from the Earth. At these times, the Moon's apparent diameter will be reduced, and consequently the solar disc will not be completely covered. The Sun remains visible as a bright ring around the lunar disc. The term 'annular' is derived from the Latin word *annulus* meaning *ring*.

Mainly because the Earth is rotating, the Moon's shadow sweeps across the Earth's surface during a solar eclipse. The route taken by the umbra is called the 'path of totality'. For an observer in the path of totality, the Sun will temporarily pass completely behind the Moon and a total solar eclipse will take place. However, only part of the Sun will be obscured from within the penumbra — observers in the penumbral regions seeing only a partial eclipse.

Solar eclipses occur at new Moon, and lunar eclipses at full Moon. However, eclipses do not occur every month. There are a maximum of three lunar eclipses in any one year, while the maximum number of solar eclipses is five. Solar eclipses can be seen only from areas within or near the path of totality, although lunar eclipses are visible from anywhere on the hemisphere facing the Moon at the time. Therefore, for any particular location on the Earth, lunar eclipses are much more common than solar eclipses.

Below: *Solar eclipses give astronomers the chance of studying the outer layers of the Sun's atmosphere. This eclipse seen from Mexico, on 7 March 1970, was observed by scientists from fourteen nations. They photographed the Sun's corona. It appears as a halo around the obscured disc of the Sun.*

SOLAR ECLIPSES UNTIL AD 2000

Date	Type of eclipse	Area from which eclipse will be visible
22 July 1990	Total	Finland, USSR, Pacific Ocean
15/16 Jan 1991	Annular	Australia, New Zealand, Pacific Ocean
11 July 1991	Total	Pacific Ocean, Central America, Brazil
4/5 Jan 1992	Annular	Central Pacific Ocean
30 June 1992	Total	South Atlantic Ocean
24 Dec 1992	Partial	Arctic
21 May 1993	Partial	Arctic
13 Nov 1993	Partial	Antarctic
10 May 1994	Annular	Pacific Ocean, Mexico, USA, Canada, Atlantic Ocean
3 Nov 1994	Total	Peru, Brazil, South Atlantic Ocean
29 Apr 1995	Annular	South Pacific Ocean, Peru, Brazil, South Atlantic Ocean
24 Oct 1995	Total	Iran, India, East Indies, Pacific Ocean
17 Apr 1996	Partial	Antarctic
12 Oct 1996	Partial	Arctic
9 Mar 1997	Total	USSR, Arctic Ocean
2 Sep 1997	Partial	Antarctic
26 Feb 1998	Total	Pacific Ocean, Atlantic Ocean
22 Aug 1998	Annular	Indian Ocean, East Indies, Pacific Ocean
16 Feb 1999	Annular	Indian Ocean, Australia, Pacific Ocean
11 Aug 1999	Total	Atlantic Ocean, England, France, Central Europe, Turkey, India

MERCURY AND VENUS

Mercury is the innermost planetary member of the solar system, orbiting the Sun once every 88 days at an average distance of 36 million miles (58 million km). Venus is the second planet out from the Sun which it orbits every 225 days at an average distance of 67 million miles (108 million km).

Mercury

Mercury is usually seen low over the horizon (because it is so close to the Sun), either in the East before sunrise or in the West after sunset. Needless to say, the fact that Mercury is never seen against a truly dark sky has made observation from Earth very difficult.

Before the space age, our entire knowledge of Mercury was gleaned from observations made under these conditions. The Italian astronomer Giovanni Virginio Schiaparelli was the first to try and map the surface of the planet. Between 1881 and 1889, he recorded numerous light and dark areas and produced a chart that was rough and unenlightening to say the least. The Greek astronomer Eugenios Antoniadi published a more informative chart in 1934.

It was not until the 1970s that the surface of Mercury was finally revealed to us. In November 1973, the American Mariner 10 craft was launched and it made the first ever fly-by of Mercury in March 1974. This was followed by further passes in September 1974 and March 1975, and we consequently have detailed maps of some of the Mercurian surface. The Mariner 10 cameras revealed craters, mountains, ridges and valleys on Mercury's surface and showed it to be comparable in many ways to the Moon,

Heat loss

Although the temperature at Mercury's surface can be as high as 800°F (425°C) on the equator at noon, this can plummet to a frigid −300°F (−180°C) just before sunrise. The main reason for this immense difference in temperature is the virtual lack of an insulating atmosphere around the planet. The Earth's atmosphere retains much of the heat received from the Sun during the day, preventing such a dramatic reduction at night.

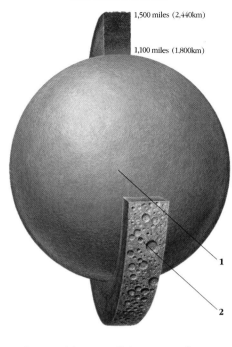

1,500 miles (2,440km)

1,100 miles (1,800km)

1

2

Below: *Until the 1970s all observations of Mercury were made from Earth. In 1974 the American spaceprobe Mariner 10 gave us our first detailed views. It made a series of television pictures covering 40 per cent of Mercury's surface.*

Left: *The craters on Mercury's surface make it look like the Moon, but the interior is very different. Mercury's density almost equals that of Earth, even though Mercury is only one third the size. This suggests Mercury is made of a heavy material such as iron. In fact 70-80 per cent of the planet is an iron core (1) making Mercury twice as rich in iron as any other solar system planet. The outer region (2) is made of silicate rock, like the Earth's mantle. The surface of Mercury is more complex than the Moon's but followed a similar evolutionary path of meteorite bombardment, followed by volcanism.*

although there were fewer of the dark plains that dominate the lunar surface.

The largest of the dark plains discovered on Mercury was the Caloris Basin an 812 miles (1,300km) diameter feature surrounded by mountainous regions reaching up to 1·25 miles (2km) above the Mercurian surface. Unfortunately, only half of the Caloris Basin was actually photographed by Mariner 10, which makes our knowledge of this impressive feature and the rest of Mercury somewhat incomplete. As well as being similar in appearance to the Moon, the diameters of the two bodies are also comparable — the diameter of Mercury being 3,032 miles (4,880km).

Both Schiaparelli and Antoniadi thought that Mercury had a captured rotation in that it would keep one hemisphere permanently facing the Sun throughout its orbit. This would mean that Mercury's orbital period ('year') and axial rotation period ('day') would be equal, and that half of the planet would experience permanent daylight and the other permanent night. However, we now know that Mercury spins once on its axis every 58·65 days resulting in all the Mercurian surface receiving sunlight at one time or another. This does mean, however, that Mercury spins exactly three times during two revolutions of the Sun meaning that the Mercurian solar day (sunrise to sunrise) is two Mercurian years long!

Although Antoniadi believed that he had seen clouds above the surface of Mercury, it is now known that the Mercurian atmosphere is far too thin to support them. Mariner 10 did detect small amounts of hydrogen and helium near Mercury's surface, although the most abundant component of the atmosphere seems to be sodium. However, Mercury's atmosphere is so thin that it is more rarefied than the best vacuum produced in a laboratory on Earth.

Above: *Mariner 10 took this view of Venus while on its way to Mercury. It shows the dense layer of cloud which permanently covers the planet. But the clouds are not like Earth's; these are made of sulphuric acid and chlorine compounds.*

Venus

Venus spins once on its axis every 243 days giving Venus a 'day' that is longer than its 'year'! Like Mercury, Venus orbits the Sun inside the orbit of Earth and is seen only in the eastern sky before sunrise or in the West after sunset. However, because Venus is further away from the Sun, it can remain in the sky for a longer period and is often seen against a dark sky.

Venus is the closest planet to Earth and is the brightest object in the sky, apart from the Sun and Moon. This brilliance is due to a covering of dense white clouds which reflect three-quarters of the sunlight received by the planet. However, as well as making Venus a beautiful naked-eye sight, the clouds permanently hide the surface of the planet preventing us from seeing anything more than the cloud tops.

The main component of the Venusian atmosphere is carbon dioxide, although traces of many other materials have been found including carbon monoxide, water vapour and sulphur dioxide. Although it is around 150 miles (250km) deep, most of the atmosphere is concentrated within 17 miles

3,750 miles (6,050km)

1,900 miles (3,100km)

1

2

3

4

Above: *Venus is second only to the Moon in the number of visits it has received from spacecraft. Below its thick atmosphere (4) is a surface hot enough to melt lead, with an atmospheric pressure nearly one hundred times as great as Earth's. The first pictures showing a rocky terrain were sent by the Russian Venera craft in 1975. Below this rocky crust (3) Venus is believed to have a mantle (2) and an iron/silicate core (1).*

Right: *Venus has phases like Earth's Moon. Its visibility and*

the phases it shows depend on its position relative to the Earth's as they orbit the Sun.

(28km) of the surface. This produces a phenomenal surface pressure of around 90 times that of the Earth! The thick atmosphere has also created a runaway 'greenhouse effect' — the heat which filters down to the surface of the planet from the Sun is unable to escape back into space. This has produced a surface temperature of well over 740°F (400°C)!

While we cannot actually 'see' through the Venusian atmosphere, special mapping techniques used by space probes have enabled us to chart most of the surface. This technique is known as radar mapping and has been used by both American and Soviet space probes. Radar pulses are transmitted through the atmosphere to bounce off the surface below and back to the waiting craft. The length of time it takes for the signal to return is plotted, enabling the actual distance the signal has travelled to be worked out. For example, if the radar pulse hits a mountain peak it will have less distance to travel, and will therefore rebound to the orbiting probe in less time, than if it had hit a valley floor.

Radar mapping has shown us that flat rolling plains occupy most of the Venusian surface. There are several highland regions including Aphrodite Terra — an area about the size of Africa which straddles the equator — and Ishtar Terra — roughly the size of Australia and situated further to the North. Ishtar Terra contains a number of mountains including Maxwell Montes which, at a height of 7 miles (11km), is the highest mountain on Venus. By comparison, the deepest valley on Venus is Diana Chasma. With a width of almost 180 miles (300km) and a maximum depth of around 1·25 miles (2km), Diana Chasma is comparable in size to Valles Marineris on Mars.

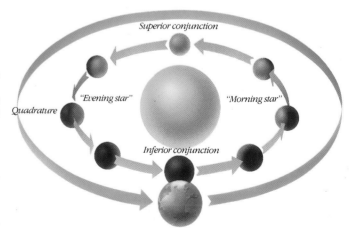

Superior conjunction

"Evening star"

"Morning star"

Quadrature

Inferior conjunction

MARS

Mars is the outermost of the terrestrial planets, orbiting the Sun once every 687 days at an average distance of 141 million miles (228 million km). Its distance from the Sun varies somewhat due to the eccentric orbit of Mars. At its closest point to Earth, the planet comes to within 128·4 million miles (206·7 million km) moving out to 154·9 million miles (249·1 million km) at its furthest point.

The conspicuous red colour of Mars caused it to be named after the God of War. This coloration is due to reddish dust scattered across vast areas of the Martian surface. Winds that sweep across the surface sometimes lift this dust high into the tenuous Martian atmosphere creating huge dust clouds that can hide vast areas of the planet from view.

Past observers

Many famous astronomers have turned their telescopes towards the Red Planet — notably William Herschel who found that the tilt of Mars' axis of rotation is very similar to that of the Earth (24° as opposed to 23·5° for our planet). As a result the Martian seasons are similar to those on the Earth, although they last longer as Mars takes nearly twice as long to travel around the Sun.

Surface markings were first seen on Mars by the Dutch astronomer Christiaan Huygens in 1659, when he observed the triangular dark feature known today as the large plateau Syrtis Major. When Huygens observed how quickly Syrtis Major appeared to cross the Martian disc, he estimated a rotation period of 24 hours for Mars. This value was improved upon by the Italian astronomer Giovanni Domenico Cassini a few years later. He determined the Martian axial rotation period to be almost 37·5 minutes longer than the Earth's. Cassini was also the first to report the existence of the Martian polar ice caps — now known to contain frozen water.

The Martian canals

One of the better-known observers of the Red Planet was the American astronomer Percival Lowell. In 1877, the Italian astronomer Giovanni Schiaparelli reported seeing a number of linear features crossing the Martian surface. He called them *canali* — an Italian word indicating natural channels. Yet for some reason the word became incorrectly translated as *canals* — waterways that are created artificially!

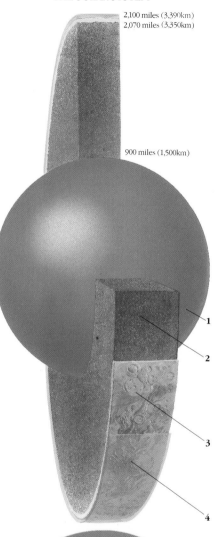

2,100 miles (3,390km)
2,070 miles (3,350km)

900 miles (1,500km)

1
2
3
4

Left: Mars is generally believed to have a core (1), mantle (2) and crust (3) but the exact thickness of each layer is unknown. The core is probably smaller and cooler than Earth's. The mantle was the source of the lava which went into the building of the Tharsis highland. The Tharsis 'bulge' is a crease in the crust where Olympus Mons, Mars' largest volcano, is found. The surface crust also includes crater-scarred plains, rift valleys and canyons. Above its surface Mars has a thin atmosphere which has only one-hundredth the surface pressure of the Earth's.

Above right: Two American Viking landers touched down on Mars in 1976. Viking 1 used its robot arm to collect and analyse rock samples. Aluminium, silicon, calcium, iron, carbon dioxide and water were detected, but no organic material.

Below: A modern observational map of Syrtis Major compared with (left) Lowell's drawing of the region in which he identified 'canals'.

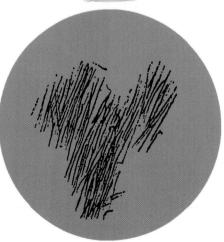

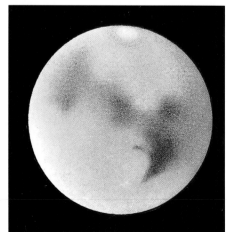

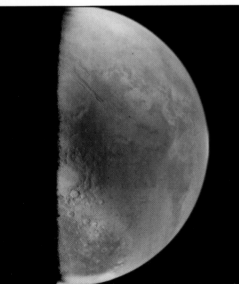

Above: *While the Viking lander craft investigated Mars's surface, the Viking Orbiters travelled around the planet. They orbited close enough to image features 330 feet (100 m) across. The enormous Argyre impact basin is shown here (bottom).*

probe consisted of a lander and an orbiter — both landers making successful landings in 1976. Viking 1 touched down at 22° North, in a rocky area known as Chryse Planitia, north of the Martian equator. Viking 2 landed further to the north and almost on the opposite side of the planet in Utopia Planitia. The Viking landers carried out a great deal of useful work including the monitoring of the Martian atmosphere and weather changes and the transmission of over 4,500 photographs. These showed, amongst other things, that the Martian sky had a reddish tint, caused by fine dust suspended in the atmosphere. The atmospheric content was found to be mainly carbon dioxide — the surface pressure being less than 1 per cent that of the Earth at sea level. The temperature at the Martian surface was found to range from a minimum just before sunrise to a maximum shortly after midday.

Martian features

It is believed that water exists on Mars, additional to that in the polar ice caps. This may be in the form of permafrost, locked up under the Martian surface. Certainly there is no liquid running across the Martian surface today, although evidence for this in the past was obtained from Mariner 9, which detected features that looked very much like dried-up river beds. Among the 51,500 images sent back by the Viking orbiters were pictures of what appeared to be areas eroded by huge floods of water. This water may have come up from below the surface after impacts by meteorites. The heat generated by these impacts may have melted the ice beneath the surface, producing flash floods which sent vast torrents of water across the surrounding terrain.

Mars has many prominent features including the spectacular Valles Marineris — a vast network of valleys stretching away from the area to the east of the Tharsis region. Valles Marineris was discovered by (and named after) the Mariner 9 spacecraft, and stretches over 2,500 miles (4,000km), running more or less parallel to the equator.

The Tharsis region is a highland area containing a number of large shield volcanoes, the biggest of which (and the largest in the Solar System) is Olympus Mons. This huge feature towers 15 miles (25km) over the Martian surface and has a diameter at its base of over 370 miles (600km). Its summit crater, or caldera, is 50 miles (80km) across. Olympus Mons dwarfs even the largest volcanoes on Earth.

Soon, many astronomers (and other people) got the idea that an intelligent Martian civilisation was irrigating areas of the planet by transferring water from the polar ice caps using huge canal systems! Lowell was just one of a number of astronomers who 'discovered' more Martian canals — Lowell himself charting over 150. However, their existence has been well and truly disproved, primarily through the use of space probes.

Exploration of Mars by space probe

In July 1965, the American Mariner 4 craft flew past Mars, sending back various data including 21 pictures — it became the first successful Mars probe. The pictures showed numerous features including craters. Several astronomers had already reported seeing craters on Mars, and Mariner 4 offered proof of these observations. Mariners 6 and 7 flew past the planet in 1969, returning over 200 pictures. In November 1971, Mariner 9 went into orbit around Mars, and during the following 11 months sent back well over 7,000 images before contact was lost in October 1972.

The two American Viking probes were successfully launched to Mars in 1975. Each

THE ASTEROIDS

In 1766, the German mathematician, Johann Titius, noticed that the values of the distances of the planets from the Sun were linked by a sequence of numbers. This sequence showed that there should have been a planet orbiting the Sun between Mars and Jupiter. In fact, if you look at any scale drawing of the Solar System, you will see that there is a large gap between the orbits of these two planets. Titius suggested that there must be an undiscovered planet orbiting the Sun in this area. He was not the first to put forward this idea, and as long ago as 1596, the German astronomer Johannes Kepler suggested that this region may play host to an extra member of the Sun's family.

At first astronomers were sceptical. However in 1772, another German astronomer, Johann Bode, revived and publicised the idea. This, together with the discovery of Uranus by William Herschel in 1781, did much to sway opinion. Uranus was found to tie in well with Titius' sequence of numbers.

The celestial police

Suddenly, astronomers began to think that Titius may be right and that there was indeed a 'missing planet' waiting to be discovered. In 1800, Johann Schröter called together a group of astronomers at his observatory in Lilienthal, Germany, with the purpose of organising a search for the planet. Among those present were the Hungarian observer Baron Franz Xavier von Zach, and the Germans Heinrich Olbers ànd Karl Harding. They christened themselves the Celestial Police and decided to split the zodiac (the region of sky through which the planets move) into a number of areas, each of which would be searched by more than one astronomer. Schröter and his team could not hope to do this alone, and requests for help were sent out to other observers.

The search for the asteroids

The first asteroid (minor planet) was actually discovered by the Italian astronomer Giuseppe Piazzi, on 1st January 1801. Observing the sky from the Palermo Observatory in Sicily, where he was Director, Piazzi was plotting the positions of stars so that he could include them in his new star catalogue. During his observations, he noticed an 8th magnitude object in Taurus which was not on any of the other star charts available at the time. A few nights later, he noticed that the object had

Right: *The asteroid belt, shown here as the wide orange band, lies between the orbits of Mars and Jupiter. But not all asteroids lie in this belt. They travel in orbits of low eccentricity, between about 2.2 and 3.5 astronomical units from the Sun. The Hilda group, a much smaller group, orbit at about 4 astronomical units. Other asteroids are found in the same orbit as Jupiter, but either preceding or following the planet by around 60. These are the Trojans. A few asteroids, like Apollo, have eccentric orbits which bring them closer to the Sun than Earth.*

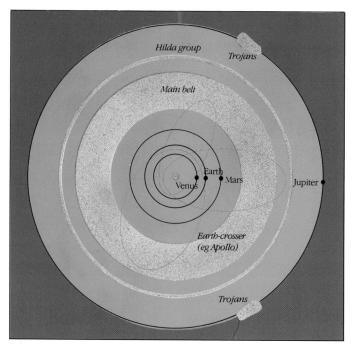

changed position and he wrote to von Zach to tell him about the discovery. However, by the time von Zach received the letter, the object had moved behind the Sun and disappeared from view.

Von Zach was sure that Piazzi had found the missing planet; although when it eventually came out from behind the Sun nobody would know where to look for it! The brilliant German mathematician, Karl Gauss, calculated an orbit for the object from the few observations available and predicted when and where it would reappear. In December, von Zach spotted it almost exactly where

Below: *The first asteroid, Ceres, was discovered by Giuseppe Piazzi in 1801. The frontispiece of his star catalogue commemorates this discovery.*

Above: *In this night sky photograph the stars are shown as pinpoints of light. The three dashes are the trails of minor planets. Their movement, with respect to the stars, was caught by the camera.*

Right: *This medal commemorates the work of three astronomers who together discovered 41 asteroids.*

Gauss had said it would be. The orbital distance was found to be 257 million miles (412 million km), tying in well with Titius' sequence of numbers. Piazzi named the new planet Ceres, after the Roman goddess of corn and harvests, and who is also the patron saint of Sicily.

Ceres turned out to be quite small when compared to the rest of the planets. The Celestial Police decided that there must be other objects in the same region of sky and so they continued their search. In 1802, Olbers discovered a second asteroid, Pallas, which was also found to lie between Mars and Jupiter.

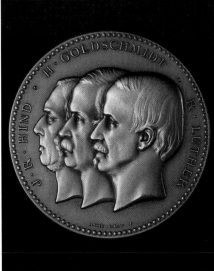

Olbers suggested that both these small objects were once part of a much larger planet that broke up long ago. Karl Harding found a third asteroid, Juno, in 1804, this being followed by the discovery of Vesta by Olbers in 1807. After this, no more asteroids were found and the Celestial Police organisation disbanded in 1815.

The next discovery was that of Astraea by the German Karl Hencke in 1845, following his 15 year search for further asteroids in the region of sky 15° to either side of the celestial equator. He had further success when he discovered the sixth asteroid, Hebe, in July 1847. Asteroids 7 (Iris) and 8 (Flora) were discovered by the Englishman John Russel Hind later in 1847; and since then every year has seen further discoveries being made.

Enter photography

Until the late 19th century, astronomers discovered asteroids telescopically by trying to spot points of light that changed position over a period of time. This was hard work, particularly on cold nights! However, the German astronomer, Maximilian Franz Joseph Cornelius Wolf (better known as Max Wolf), was to change all this.

Max Wolf suggested that the best way to search for asteroids was to use a camera which was made to follow the stars as they moved across the sky. Stars would appear as points of light on the photograph. However, anything that moved against the background of stars, such as an asteroid, would appear as a streak of light. He made the first photographic discovery of an asteroid in 1891, when he found Brucia, the 323rd asteroid to be discovered. The photographic method was so successful that, by 1900, the total number of known asteroids had risen to 452 – Wolf himself discovered 232 – and by 1923, over a thousand asteroids were known. It is thought that the overall total may be as high as a million!

The asteroids are all small, the largest being Ceres with a diameter of around 621 miles (1,000km); and even their combined mass would be considerably less than that of our Moon. For many years, astronomers paid these tiny objects little attention, although the general opinion now is that the study of the asteroids may tell us much about the early history of the Solar System. Asteroids were formed from debris left over from the original formation of the Solar System. Through their observation, we may yet unlock some of the long-hidden secrets of our celestial neighbourhood.

19

JUPITER

Jupiter is a huge world with a mass 318 times that of the Earth. Its equatorial diameter is 89,000 miles (143,000km), which means it is over 11 times the size of our planet and the largest planet in the Solar System. So large is Jupiter that, if it were hollowed out, nearly 1,500 Earths would fit inside!

Jupiter travels around the Sun once every 11·86 years at a mean distance of 484 million miles (778 million km). It spins once on its axis in just under 10 hours. This axial rotation period is very short for a planet as large as Jupiter, causing it to become flattened by the centrifugal forces produced. Its equatorial diameter exceeds that across its poles by around 5,000 miles (8,000km), and even a small telescope will clearly show Jupiter's prominent equatorial bulge.

Inside Jupiter

Looking at Jupiter, all we can see are the outer layers of its thick atmosphere. At the centre is a rocky core on top of which is a layer of hydrogen around 25,000 miles (40,000km) thick. The pressure pushing down on this layer from the atmosphere above is so great that the hydrogen atoms are stripped of their electrons. They produce a region of so-called liquid metallic hydrogen in which all the particles, including the electrons, move around independently of each other. Above this is a layer of hydrogen some 12,500 miles (20,000km) deep, the outermost layer of which is thought to be around 625 miles

(1,000km) deep. It is the outer surface of this uppermost layer that we see when we view the planet.

Colours of Jupiter

Jupiter is one of the brightest planets and one of the four gas giants. Telescopes reveal details in its colourful and turbulent upper atmosphere; even a small telescope shows two dark belts girdling Jupiter's equatorial regions. Larger telescopes reveal many more similar features including bright zones (regions where gases are welling up from the Jovian interior to cool at the surface) and darker belts (regions where the gases are descending). The belts and zones have a wide variety of colours including red, orange, brown and yellow.

The Great Red Spot, first seen by the Italian astronomer Giovanni Cassini in 1665, is a huge oval atmospheric feature in Jupiter's

The Great Red Spot

The Great Red Spot is a colossal feature. It alters in size, sometimes reaching a length of 25,000 miles (40,000km), a width of 8,750 miles (14,000km) and a diameter over three times that of Earth! It has been observed almost continuously since it was first seen by Cassini in 1665. A feature seen by English astronomer Robert Hooke, in 1664, may have been the Great Red Spot.

Left: When viewed through a telescope Jupiter's disc appears to be crossed by dark cloud belts, and brighter bands which are known as zones. Jupiter's surface features are always changing but there are belts and zones which are relatively stable; these are shown here. North is at the top of the diagram. The Great Red Spot moves from left to right as the planet rotates. As Jupiter spins quickly, once in just under ten hours, its overall shape is oblate.

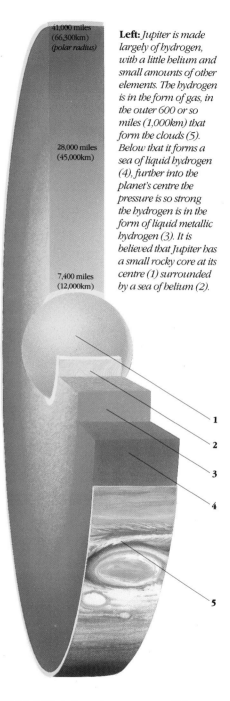

Left: Jupiter is made largely of hydrogen, with a little helium and small amounts of other elements. The hydrogen is in the form of gas, in the outer 600 or so miles (1,000km) that form the clouds (5). Below that it forms a sea of liquid hydrogen (4), further into the planet's centre the pressure is so strong the hydrogen is in the form of liquid metallic hydrogen (3). It is believed that Jupiter has a small rocky core at its centre (1) surrounded by a sea of helium (2).

41,000 miles (66,300km) (polar radius)

28,000 miles (45,000km)

7,400 miles (12,000km)

1
2
3
4
5

Right: Jupiter's ring system appears as a light orange line in this Voyager 2 false-colour image. The ring is made of very fine particles which are probably the debris from rock collisions and from eruptions on Io. The ring is thought to be no more than a few miles across.

provided a wealth of information about these worlds which, prior to the space age, were little more than points of light through the telescope. Io is an exciting world — the scene of continuous volcanic activity which was actually photographed in progess by Voyager 1 as plumes of material were ejected to heights of around 175 miles (280km)!

The smallest Galilean satellite is Europa, which is covered with a layer of water ice some 62 miles (100km) thick. Europa has been described as a fractured world, due to a number of extensive cracks running across its surface. Somewhat different are the heavily cratered surfaces of Ganymede (the largest planetary satellite in the Solar System) and Callisto, both of which also have outer crusts of water ice. One area of Ganymede, known as Galileo Regio, is a dark circular area of ancient crust containing a large number of impact craters.

Impact craters are also found strewn across the dark surface of Callisto, which is the most heavily cratered world known. One such is a large feature — the Valhalla Basin — which probably formed when an asteroid-sized object collided with Callisto a long time ago. The Valhalla Basin looks like a huge bullseye — a series of concentric rings spreading out to around 935 miles (1,500km) from the point of impact. Valhalla was formed early on in Callisto's history. We know this from seeing many other smaller craters scattered across the region — craters which were formed from more recent impacts.

The other Jovian satellites are all quite small — the outermost eight possibly being asteroids that were captured by Jupiter's gravity and pulled into orbit around the planet. The Galilean satellites, together with the other four innermost members of Jupiter's satellite family, probably formed when particles of material orbiting Jupiter collected together around the time that the planet itself was formed.

southern hemisphere. Although astronomers are undecided as to what the Great Red Spot is, it is known that a great deal of atmospheric activity is going on around it (as elsewhere on the planet).

Many of these changes have been observed through Earth-based telescopes, and spacecraft cameras have shown that the Great Red Spot rotates anticlockwise over a period of around six days. This rotation appears to be maintained by high winds blowing in opposite directions to the north and south of the Spot.

Above: *Voyager 1 took this spectacular view from a distance of 17.5 million miles. The Great Red Spot and two of Jupiter's satellites are visible. Io is against Jupiter's disc; Europa, to the planet's right. Note the planet's banded atmosphere.*

The Jovian satellites

The four largest of Jupiter's 16 satellites, Io, Europa, Ganymede and Callisto, were discovered in 1610 by the Italian astronomer Galileo and are known collectively as the Galilean satellites. The Voyayer spacecraft have

Jupiter's ring

Jupiter has a ring system, discovered by Voyager 1, which is extremely faint and cannot be seen even through the largest Earth-based telescopes. There are two sections to the ring system: an inner 3,125 mile (5,000km) wide ring, and a brighter, but narrower 500 mile (800km) ring outside it. The rings are only about half a mile thick and are made up of tiny particles which orbit Jupiter every six hours or so. The rings stretch out to over 31,250 miles (50,000km) above the top of the Jovian atmosphere.

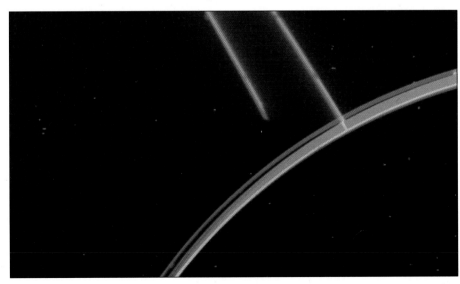

SATURN

Appearing as a yellowish starlike point of light to the naked eye, Saturn is beautiful viewed through a telescope. Even small telescopes will reveal Saturn's stunning ring system and present the observer with a sight never to be forgotten. Although many pictures of Saturn have been published, there is little to compare with actually observing it against the backdrop of a velvet-black sky.

A world that would float!

Until the discovery of Uranus in 1781, Saturn was the outermost known planet. It orbits the Sun once every 29.46 years at an average distance of 887 million miles (1,427 million km). Saturn's mass is over 95 times that of the Earth and it outweighs all the other planets put together (with the exception of Jupiter). However, in spite of its mass, Saturn has a very low density when compared to the other planets. In other words, 1 cu in (16.5 cu cm) of Saturn would weigh less than the same amount of any of the other worlds in our Solar System. This volume of Saturnian material would weigh just 0.4oz (11.5g), which is less than the density of water. This means that, given a large enough container, Saturn would float!

Saturn has an equatorial diameter of 75,000 miles (120,660km). It rotates quickly on its axis, the length of the Saturnian 'day' being just 10hr 13min 59sec at the equator. This rapid rotation has given Saturn a very oblate appearance. The polar diameter is only 67,000 miles (108,600km).

Inside Saturn

The outermost layer of Saturn comprises hydrogen, beneath which is a region of liquid metallic hydrogen. A rocky core, somewhat larger than that of Jupiter, is believed to lie at the centre of the planet. The outer visible layer of Saturn's atmosphere is traversed by dark belts and bright zones, although these are not as colourful as those of Jupiter. There is a smaller percentage of helium in Saturn's atmosphere than that of Jupiter. This may be a result of Saturn cooling down more quickly than Jupiter. This cooling produced helium 'rain' which fell from the atmosphere in towards the inner regions of the planet, leaving a reduced amount in the outer layer.

Saturn's ring system

The Italian astronomer Galileo carried out the first telescopic observations of Saturn in 1610.

He was the first to see Saturn's ring system, although his crude telescopes revealed nothing more than two lumps, one on either side of the planet. The instruments were not powerful enough to discriminate the rings in their true form. However, telescopes improved as the 17th century progressed, and it was not long before the rings of Saturn were clearly revealed. In 1655, after observing the planet, the Dutch astronomer Christiaan Huygens suggested that the lumps Galileo had seen were actually a system of rings girdling the planet.

Earth-based telescopes reveal three main sections to the ring system. These are the brightest B ring, a fainter A ring and a dim C ring, also known as the Crêpe Ring. The A and B rings are divided by the Cassini Division, a gap discovered in 1675 by the Italian astronomer Giovanni Domenico Cassini

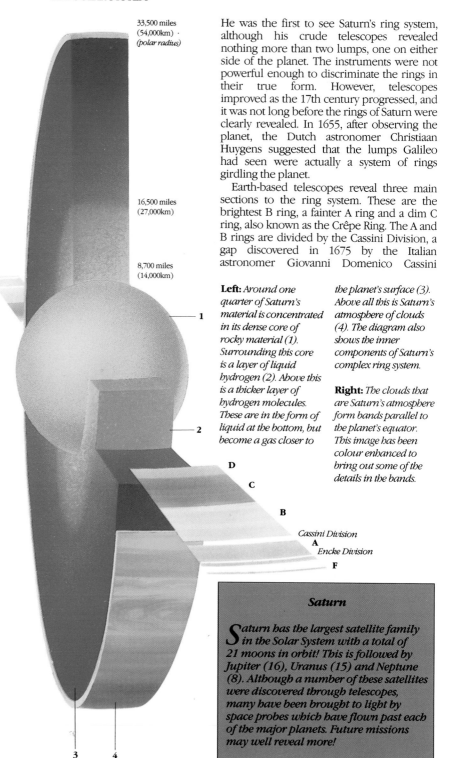

33,500 miles (54,000km) · (polar radius)

16,500 miles (27,000km)

8,700 miles (14,000km)

1

2

D

C

B

Cassini Division
A
Encke Division

F

3   4

Left: Around one quarter of Saturn's material is concentrated in its dense core of rocky material (1). Surrounding this core is a layer of liquid hydrogen (2). Above this is a thicker layer of hydrogen molecules. These are in the form of liquid at the bottom, but become a gas closer to the planet's surface (3). Above all this is Saturn's atmosphere of clouds (4). The diagram also shows the inner components of Saturn's complex ring system.

Right: The clouds that are Saturn's atmosphere form bands parallel to the planet's equator. This image has been colour enhanced to bring out some of the details in the bands.

Saturn

Saturn has the largest satellite family in the Solar System with a total of 21 moons in orbit! This is followed by Jupiter (16), Uranus (15) and Neptune (8). Although a number of these satellites were discovered through telescopes, many have been brought to light by space probes which have flown past each of the major planets. Future missions may well reveal more!

Above: *Saturn's smallest satellite is Mimas. Its icy surface is heavily cratered making it appear like a heavily dimpled golf ball.*

Below: *Enceladus, which is made of rock and ice, reveals its complex history in its surface. Some areas are smooth, others cratered.*

(who also discovered four of Saturn's moons). Another division of the ring system visible from Earth is Encke's Division. This lies in A ring and was first noted by the German astronomer Johann Encke, a scientist also famous for predicting the return of the comet that is named after him (see Comets). Encke's Division is less conspicuous than the Cassini Division.

The rings are made up of millions of tiny particles; their different brightnesses are due to the different composition in each section. Ring B contains much reflective ice, and rock particles; as a result it reflects sunlight better than its neighbours, and therefore appears brighter. Space probes have revealed that each of the main sections of the ring system is actually made up of thousands of narrow ringlets and gaps.

In 1979, Pioneer 11 discovered the F ring, which was studied in more detail by the later Voyager probes. The F ring is only 65 miles (100km) wide and contains a number of intertwined strands. The reasons for this are not known. The Voyager probes discovered the innermost D ring, which lies inside the Crêpe Ring, and the outermost G and E rings, both of which are extremely faint and contain little structure.

The satellites

Titan is the largest of Saturn's 21 satellites, with a diameter of 3,200 miles (5,150km). Titan has an atmosphere which is so thick that it completely hides the surface from view. The Voyager probes showed that nitrogen was the most abundant gas, followed by methane and argon.

The surface atmospheric pressure and temperature on Titan are such that methane may exist as a gas, liquid or solid. Such a situation exists on Earth, although instead of methane it is water which is found in gas (steam), liquid and solid (ice) forms. Titan may play host to methane lakes, rivers and seas fed by methane rain and snow. This has yet to be confirmed, although the joint ESA/NASA Cassini mission to Saturn, due to arrive at the planet just after the turn of the century, may provide proof. The mission includes a probe, named Huygens, which is due to descend through Titan's atmosphere to transmit results both during the descent and from the surface.

Many of the satellites have been examined with a resolution equal to the best Earth-based observation of the Moon seen through a telescope. Apart from Titan, there are a further six reasonably large satellites, these being Phoebe, Mimas, Enceladus, Tethys, Iapetus and Rhea. The other 14 satellites are all considerably smaller, and most are irregularly shaped worlds.

23

URANUS

Uranus is a giant gas planet made up mainly of hydrogen and helium. It was discovered by the amateur astronomer, William Herschel, towards the end of the eighteenth century and was the first planet to be found after the dawn of history.

William Herschel discovers Uranus

Born in Hanover, Germany, on 15th November 1738, William Herschel came to London in 1757 to earn his living as a musician. He had little success finding work in London and so toured the north of England. He was eventually offered the post of organist at the new Octagon Chapel at Bath, and in 1766 he took up his new position.

After reading a book called *Opticks* by Robert Smith (who had also written a book on harmonics), Herschel's desire to learn more about astronomy was kindled and his interest in the heavens began to take a hold. Smith's book contained an illustrated section on astronomy and it was this that stirred Herschel to observe the sky for himself.

At first, astronomy was only a hobby, and Herschel was content to teach and practise music by day and observe the sky by night, using telescopes that he had constructed himself. Yet astronomy began to take up more and more of his time, and in 1781 an event took place that was to prove the turning point in William's life.

On 13th March 1781, Herschel was looking at stars in Gemini when he spotted an object that seemed anything but starlike in appearance. The stars are so far away that even with the most powerful telescopes they appear as nothing more than points of light. However, using higher magnifications, Herschel saw that the object had a definite disc. Over the following evenings, he also noticed that it was actually moving across the sky.

At first Herschel thought that he had discovered a comet, the idea that he had actually stumbled across a new planet did not occur to him! Yet, once the orbit of the newly discovered body had been worked out, it became clear that he had indeed discovered a seventh planetary member of the Solar System, orbiting the Sun at around twice the distance of Saturn! Uranus, as the new planet came to be known, had actually been seen prior to this discovery, although it had always been mistaken for a star!

Up until the time of Uranus' discovery, Saturn had been reckoned the outermost

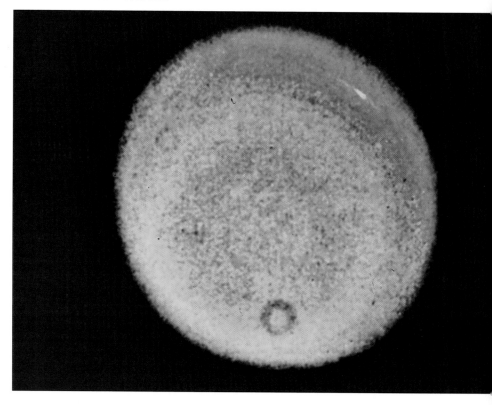

Above: *Voyager 2 flew by Uranus in January 1986 and gave us our first close-up views. But the hydrogen in its upper atmosphere scattered the sunlight that reaches the planet and prevented the cameras from seeing beneath this layer.*

known planet. Now, thanks to Herschel's skills as an observer, the size of the known Solar System had doubled! Uranus was the first planet to be discovered telescopically; all the other planets known at the time being prominent to the naked eye and known since antiquity.

The planet Uranus

The diameter of Uranus is 31,572 miles (50,800km) and it orbits the Sun once every 84·01 years at a mean distance of 1,784 million miles (2,870 million km). It spins once on its axis every 17hr 12min.

The axial tilt of Uranus is just under 98°, meaning that its axis of rotation is almost lined up with the plane of its orbit around the Sun. Why Uranus should have such an unusual tilt is not known, although it does produce weird effects on the Uranian days and seasons. At certain times in the Uranian 'year', its north and south poles point almost at the Sun, while at other times, the Sun is high over the equator. Our view of Uranus changes somewhat. If either its north or south pole is tilted towards the Sun, we look down on the planet's polar regions. At other times we gaze onto its equator.

Satellites and rings

Uranus has 15 satellites, 10 of which were discovered by Voyager 2 in 1986. The largest is Titania, found by William Herschel in 1787, which has a diameter of 1,000 miles (1,600km). In the same year Herschel also discovered Oberon, followed by Umbriel in 1802. The other two large satellites are Miranda and Ariel. The diameters of the 10 satellites found by Voyager are all in the order of a few tens of miles.

On 10th March 1977, Uranus passed in front of a star. Astronomers were keen to watch this event as observation of the star fading as it passed behind the planet could tell us something about Uranus' atmosphere. However, a surprise was in store. Shortly before the star was due to disappear behind Uranus, its light was seen to fade several times. After it reappeared, a similar sequence of 'fadings' was seen on the other side of the planet. This could only mean one thing —

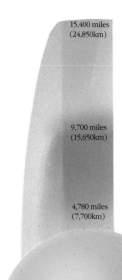

15,400 miles (24,850km)

9,700 miles (15,650km)

4,780 miles (7,700km)

Left: *Uranus's core (1) may be composed of rocky material, ammonia, methane and water, mixed in with hydrogen and helium, with clouds of ammonia and water ice above (2). Its outer layer (3) is of hydrogen and helium gas, with methane. The blue-green colour of the atmosphere comes from methane gas reflecting sunlight.*

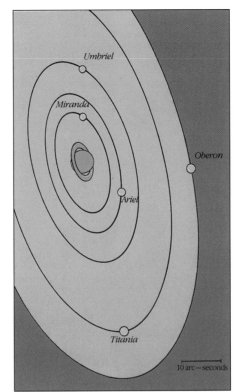

Umbriel

Miranda

Oberon

Ariel

Titania

10 arc—seconds

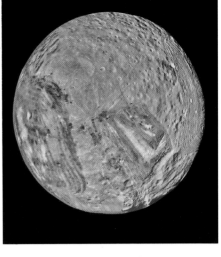

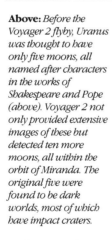

Above: *Miranda has one of the strangest landscapes in the solar system. Much of its surface is covered in craters. Parallel ridges and grooves cut across this and three oval land-forms have been found.*

Below: *Titania at around 982 miles (1,580km) in diameter is the largest Uranian moon. Its surface is covered in impact craters. The long and deep fault valleys are also easy to see.*

Above: *Before the Voyager 2 flyby, Uranus was thought to have only five moons, all named after characters in the works of Shakespeare and Pope (above). Voyager 2 not only provided extensive images of these but detected ten more moons, all within the orbit of Miranda. The original five were found to be dark worlds, most of which have impact craters.*

there was a ring system girdling Uranus. Observations made since then, together with images returned by Voyager 2, have revealed the total number of rings to be 11. The ring system circles Uranus between 26,100 and 32,300 miles (42,000 and 52,000km) from the centre of the planet.

Observing Uranus

Although Uranus had not been recognised as a planet until 1781, it can, when suitably placed, become bright enough to be visible to the naked eye. However, its maximum magnitude is only 5·6 meaning that exceptionally clear skies and keen eyesight are required to glimpse it without binoculars or a telescope. It also helps if you know exactly where to look! There is little surprise therefore that the planet remained hidden until Herschel's fortuitous discovery.

Through binoculars or a small telescope, Uranus appears as a greenish point of light, larger telescopes showing a tiny disc. Picking the planet out can be difficult, especially against the starfields of the Milky Way, and a good finder chart is essential. As with the rest of the planets, Uranus appears to move against the background of stars as it travels along its orbit, giving itself away to the careful nightly observer.

NEPTUNE

After the discovery of Uranus astronomers believed that our knowledge of the Solar System was complete, although further discoveries were in store. Observations of Uranus made during the years following its discovery revealed that it was straying from its predicted path. Astronomers deduced that these deviations were being caused by the gravity of another planet, orbiting the Sun even further out, which was 'tugging' at Uranus.

The discovery of Neptune

The young English astronomer and mathematician, John Couch Adams, decided to try and work out where the as-yet-undiscovered planet may be. He used the deviations between the predicted positions of Uranus and the actual observed positions to identify the new planet's whereabouts. After many months of work he decided that he had fixed the position accurately, and sent his results and predictions to George Biddell Airy, the Astronomer Royal at the time. Unfortunately, Airy took no action.

Unknown to Adams, the French mathematician, Urbain Jean Joseph Le Verrier, had calculated an almost identical position for the new planet by using a method similar to that of Adams. Le Verrier's predictions were sent to the Berlin Observatory where, in 1846, Johann Galle and Heinrich D'Arrest quickly located the planet in almost the exact position predicted by Le Verrier. Although it was Le Verrier's calculations that were eventually used to find Neptune, both Adams and Le Verrier are credited equally for their efforts in working out where the new planet was situated.

Neptune

Visible through large telescopes as a pale bluish disc, Neptune is the eighth planet out from the Sun. It is almost a twin of Uranus, being slightly smaller with a diameter of just 30,350 miles (48,600km). It rotates once on its axis every 17hr 50min and it orbits the Sun every 164·79 years in an almost circular path. Its average distance from the Sun is 2,795 million miles (4,497 million km). Neptune is so far away that the radio signals from the Voyager 2 space probe, which flew past the planet in August 1989, took just over four hours to reach Earth!

As the Voyager 2 space probe passed Neptune, its cameras revealed a wide variety of cloud features. Particularly prominent were

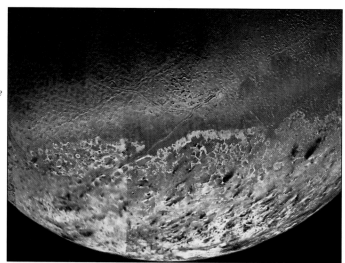

Right: *Several images were used to make this picture of Triton's south polar cap. Voyager 2 travelled within 24,800 miles (40,000km) of its surface revealing a range of geological features.*

Below: *This false colour image of Neptune was one of the last full-disc photographs to be taken by Voyager 2. It shows the haze that covers the planet in a semi-transparent layer. At the planet's edge the haze scatters sunlight and produces a red image.*

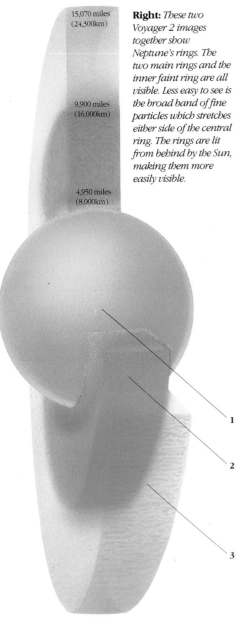

15,070 miles
(24,300km)

9,900 miles
(16,000km)

4,950 miles
(8,000km)

Right: *These two Voyager 2 images together show Neptune's rings. The two main rings and the inner faint ring are all visible. Less easy to see is the broad band of fine particles which stretches either side of the central ring. The rings are lit from behind by the Sun, making them more easily visible.*

Above: *Neptune's makeup is similar to that of Uranus; it is mostly hydrogen and helium with lesser amounts of methane and other gases. But the smaller Neptune contains more, densely-packed, material. Its central core (1) is surrounded by an icy layer of water, methane and ammonia (2). Its outer atmosphere (3) is of hydrogen and helium. Clouds of methane gas and ice crystals make the planet look blue-green.*

Then there were four

The discovery of a Neptunian ring system has shown that all the four gas giants (Jupiter, Saturn, Uranus and Neptune) have ring systems. Before space probes visited the outer planets, it was originally widely believed that Saturn was the only planet that possessed a ring system.

bright polar collars and broad bands in different shades of blue girdling Neptune's southern hemisphere. The most remarkable cloud feature seen was a huge oval storm cloud roughly the size of Earth. It has been named the Great Dark Spot, and is similar in many ways to the Great Red Spot on Jupiter. Cirrus-type clouds of frozen methane were seen forming and changing shape above and around the Great Dark Spot. Another bright cloud feature seen by Voyager 2 was 'The Scooter', so called because it was seen to travel around the planet at a quicker rate than the other clouds. Beneath the visible atmosphere, Neptune is thought to consist of a layer of melted ice surrounding a rocky core.

Satellites and rings

Prior to the Voyager 2 encounter, only two satellites were known to orbit Neptune. The Voyager cameras revealed that the true figure is eight. The largest of these is Triton, which has a diameter of 1,700 miles (2,720km) and orbits Neptune once every 5·88 days in an east to west (retrograde) direction. Its surface has

lots of interesting features including fault lines and a bright polar region. This area reflects around 90 per cent of the sunlight it receives.

Only a few craters were seen on Triton, which suggests that the surface of this remarkable satellite may be fairly young on the geological time scale, perhaps less than 500 million years. It has even been suggested that Triton may still be volcanically active. Dark streaks seen near the south pole may be formed from liquid nitrogen being thrown up into the atmosphere to heights of several tens of miles, becoming frozen and then being 'blown' by gentle winds and deposited across the surface. The features seen certainly resemble wind streaks spotted elsewhere in the Solar System.

Voyager 2 also spotted frozen lakes on the surface, which may have been formed by material ejected from Triton freezing in low-lying regions of the surface. Chemical reaction between solar radiation and the material on Triton's surface may have produced the pinkish colouring seen across Triton's southern hemisphere. The very thin atmosphere of Triton is comprised of methane and nitrogen and produces an atmospheric pressure at Triton's surface just 0.00001 that of the Earth at sea level.

A system of rings was found around the planet. These comprise two main rings together with a fainter inner third ring. A sheet of particles was also seen extending through part of the ring system. Although the presence of a ring system had been suggested from Earth-based observations, the Voyager 2 cameras provided confirmation of their existence.

27

PLUTO

Pluto is the smallest of the major planets in our Solar System. Because of the eccentric nature of its orbit, it sometimes enters inside the orbit of Neptune when it is near the point of closest approach to the Sun. It was discovered on 18th February, 1930 by a young astronomer called Clyde Tombaugh.

The discovery of Pluto

Even after the discovery of Neptune, astronomers noticed that Uranus was still straying from its predicted path, apparently under the gravitational pull of an undiscovered 'Planet X'. Several astronomers, including the American Percival Lowell, carried out systematic searches for a trans-Neptunian planet, although these all proved negative. Another, and extremely thorough, search was carried out by the young American astronomer Clyde Tombaugh from the Lowell Observatory in Arizona, U.S. During his search, Tombaugh took photographs of selected areas of sky, followed by repeat exposures made several nights later. Each pair of photographs was searched to see if any of the images had moved. Tombaugh's efforts were finally rewarded in 1930 when a new planet came to light.

The new planet was named Pluto, the first two letters of its name chosen as a tribute to the pioneering work of Percival Lowell. It was found to have the most eccentric orbit of any planet in the Solar System. Its average distance from the Sun is 3,667 million miles (5,900 million km) and it takes 248 years to travel once around our star. For 20 years of its orbit, Pluto crosses the orbit of Neptune, temporarily giving up its role as the outermost planet. This last happened in 1979, and until 1999 Neptune will actually be the most distant planet. Pluto is the smallest planet, with a diameter of around 1,400 miles (2,300km).

Pluto's mass is only 0·002 of the Earth's, and its density less than twice that of water, which suggests that Pluto is made up of a mixture of rock and frozen methane. This low mass means that Pluto's influence is not strong enough to cause the gravitational 'tugging' on Uranus and Neptune that Lowell and others had noticed. Only by co-incidence was Pluto near the predicted position, and the planet that Lowell predicted to account for the perturbations in Uranus' orbit may even lie beyond Pluto ... still awaiting discovery.

Left: *Little is known about Pluto's structure and composition. Its low density implies that it is almost entirely composed of water ice and frozen gases. Its surface is highly reflective and covered in frozen methane.*

Below: *Although Charon, Pluto's satellite has not yet been clearly seen, it has been established that its orbit is very steeply inclined.*

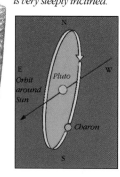

Above: *Pluto is the only planet to have been discovered photographically. These are sections of the discovery plates. The same area of sky is shown a few nights apart; 23 January 1930, left, and 29 January 1930, right. When Clyde Tombaugh looked at these plates on 18 February 1930 he saw that something had moved against the background of stars (see arrows). He had discovered Pluto.*

Subsequent observation has shown that Charon orbits Pluto at a mean distance of 12,240 miles (19,700km) over a period of 6 days 9hr and 57min. This period is identical to the rotational period of Pluto. Measurements show that Charon is around half the size of Pluto, therefore the Pluto/Charon system is more realistically regarded as a double planet rather than a planet and satellite.

As Charon moves around Pluto, it keeps the same face turned towards the planet. Also, because it orbits Pluto over a period equal to Pluto's axial rotation period, an observer standing on the surface of Pluto would see the satellite apparently suspended in the sky; never changing its position relative to the Plutonian horizon!

In many ways, both Pluto and Charon resemble the icy satellites of Jupiter and the other gas giants. It has even been suggested that Pluto may be an escaped satellite of Neptune, having been wrenched away from the planet through some cataclysmic event long ago.

Triton, the largest Neptunian satellite, has an unusual orbit in that it travels around Neptune in an east to west direction. Perhaps the same event that plucked Pluto away from Neptune also reversed Triton's orbit!

Charon

In 1978, James W. Christy of the U.S. Naval Observatory was examining photographs of Pluto when he noticed a slight 'bump' on one of the images of the planet. Similar 'bumps' were noticed on earlier photographs, and astronomers concluded that Pluto had a satellite. The satellite was named Charon.

Above: *In this artist's impression Pluto is seen with its moon, Charon, discovered in 1978. Methane clouds can be seen drifting in from the left.*

Right: *Percival Lowell, published his predictions for a new planet in 1915. His own observatory used a photographic telescope to make the search.*

Another hypothesis suggests that Pluto and Charon are merely chunks of debris left over from the formation of the planets long ago, and should be regarded as nothing more than distant asteroids! Whatever their origins, we still have a great deal to learn about the distant Pluto/Charon system.

Patience pays off!

During Tombaugh's search for a trans-Neptunian planet, he spent thousands of hours examining hundreds of pairs of photographs, which contained millions of individual star images. After the discovery of Pluto, Tombaugh continued his search for further planets beyond Neptune — no more were discovered.

COMETS

Comets can be awe-inspiring sights, although in reality they are fairly insignificant members of the Solar System. Comets are insubstantial, made up mainly of rarefied dust and gas; although the appearance of bright comets has always struck fear into the hearts of primitive peoples.

Comets are thought to originate from a vast cloud of material (Oort's Cloud) which completely surrounds the Solar System and is located beyond the orbit of Pluto.

The structure of a comet

A comet starts off as a frozen collection of gas and dust — a kind of 'dirty snowball'. However, as it approaches the warmth of the Sun, the ice in the outer layers of the comet are vaporised and a cloud, or coma, develops around the cometary nucleus. The original dirty snowball eventually becomes the cometary nucleus, hidden from our view by the surrounding coma. Solar energy acts on the material in the coma as the comet nears the Sun. The dust and gas is 'blown away' to form one or more tails. These tails are produced by the relentless force of solar energy which forces them in the opposite direction. The comet resembles a huge cosmic finger pointing at the Sun.

As the comet makes its way back to the outer reaches of the Solar System, its distance from the Sun increases, thus the effects of solar energy get less. The tail disappears, followed by the coma, leaving the icy nucleus on a lonely journey either back to Oort's Cloud or, if affected by the gravity of one of the major planets, into a much shorter orbit. The comet may then become a regular visitor to our skies!

The effects of the Sun cause comets to shed some of their material each time they pass through the inner Solar System. Comets with very short periods can be greatly affected and eventually become much fainter. This has happened to many comets, including Encke's Comet which, when first spotted a couple of centuries ago, was quite prominent. However, its 3·3 year orbital period (the shortest known cometary orbit) has led to an almost continuous barrage by solar energy, leading to the loss of most of its material into space.

Observing comets

Many comets are discovered by amateur astronomers, although the search for these objects, and for those due to reappear,

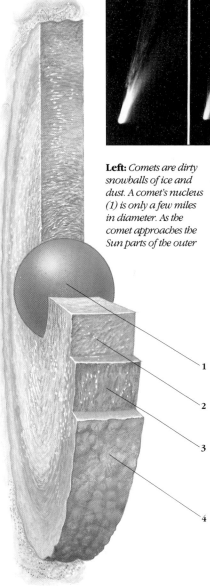

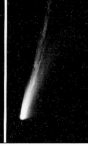

Left: *Comets are dirty snowballs of ice and dust. A comet's nucleus (1) is only a few miles in diameter. As the comet approaches the Sun parts of the outer* icy layers (2, 3) turn to gas. This gas and some of the outer dust layer (4) are blown away. They form tails which can extend tens of thousands of miles.

Above: *These pictures of Comet Mrkos were taken over a five-day period in 1957. See how the tails change. The dust tail is left, the shorter gas tail, right.*

Above: *In March 1986 the Giotto spaceprobe took the first ever photographs of a cometary nucleus.*

requires lots of patience. The observing sections of some organisations can give guidance for would-be comet searchers. The orbits of many comets are well known and their reappearance can be predicted well in advance. Many publications and organisations provide details of forthcoming cometary reappearances (see Further Information).

Comets usually appear as fuzzy patches of light when seen with a telescope, and care must be taken to make sure that the object

you are seeing is not a nebula or other deep sky object. The passage of a comet against the background of stars observed over a night or two will normally give it away.

Wide-field telescopes or good binoculars may show detail in the tail of comets — the shapes of which often change remarkably, even from night to night. Detail in the head can often be seen with higher magnifications. Their apperances may also alter as their distances from the Sun change.

METEORS AND METEORITES

Rapidly moving streaks of light may often be seen against the background of stars. These meteors (or shooting stars) are caused by tiny particles of dust, or meteoroids, which have been pulled down through the Earth's atmosphere as a result of our planet's gravitational attraction. Their speeds of entry can be anything up to 45 miles per sec (70km per sec). Collisions with air molecules heat the particles by friction, causing them to burn up and appear as shooting stars. Billions of these tiny particles are orbiting the Sun. However, they can only be seen when they destroy themselves upon entering the Earth's atmosphere.

Meteor showers

There are two kinds of meteor: shower and sporadic. Sporadic meteors can appear at any time and from any part of the sky. Shower meteors, however, are associated with comets. As a comet passes through the inner Solar System, it throws off material which forms the coma and tail. This material eventually spreads out along the comet's path. The Earth's orbit carries it through the orbital paths of certain comets at particular times of the year. When this happens, large numbers of cometary particles enter the Earth's atmosphere, producing relatively high numbers of meteors. The most famous, and active, of the annual meteor showers is the Perseids, which can be seen during July and August, and which is associated with Comet Swift-Tuttle. Each shower has a 'maximum' period, at which point the Earth is passing through the densest part of the particle swarm.

Cometary particles travel in paths parallel to one another around the comet's orbit. When they enter the atmosphere, the meteors produced will seem to come from the same point in the sky. This point is known as the radiant, and a meteor shower is named after the area of the sky in which the radiant lies. For example, the Perseid radiant lies in the constellation Perseus; the Alpha Cygnids appearing to radiate from a point near the bright star Deneb (Alpha Cygni).

The most impressive meteor shower is the Perseids, which may produce 70 or more meteors per hour at maximum (around 12th August). However, this number does not include meteors that are too faint to be seen with the naked eye, and there are many more meteors in this category.

Meteorites

These are much larger objects which survive the journey through the atmosphere without being destroyed. Fortunately, very large meteorite falls are very rare! A huge crater may be formed possibly causing a great deal of damage.

Many meteorite falls are seen each year. The paths of many can be predicted prior to entering the atmosphere. From these studies it has been revealed that many meteorites may originate in the asteroid belt, having been formed from collisions between larger bodies.

Meteor watching

Meteor watching is fairly straightforward — those wanting to take things further should get in touch with one of the national astronomical organisations. The meteor observer spends his or her time lying out under the starry sky, always making sure they are wrapped up warmly.

Although meteor showers are observed during the periods that they are active, sporadic meteors can be observed on any clear night. There are many meteor showers each year, full details of which are avaliable in various publications. If you are watching a particular shower, make a mental note of the position of the radiant in the sky before you actually start.

The times at which you start and finish your meteor watch should be noted (a meteor watch should last at least an hour, if conditions permit), as should the time at which particularly bright meteors appear.

Below: *A meteorite trail has been caught by the camera in this deep-sky view of the Milky Way.*

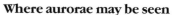

AURORAE

Deep inside the Earth, its liquid iron outer core is constantly moving around. Like a colossal dynamo, these motions create vast electrical currents which are swept outwards by the Earth's rotation. The effect of this is to produce a large magnetic field around the Earth which reaches many thousands of miles out into space.

This magnetic field is known as the magnetosphere. As the solar wind (see The Sun) hits the Earth's magnetosphere, it meets the magnetopause — the outer boundary of the magnetosphere. A shock wave is created as the movement of the energised particles, which have travelled from the Sun at speeds of around 375 miles (600km) per second, is drastically slowed down.

The Van Allen belts

The particles are usually deflected around the Earth by the magnetosheath — a turbulent region surrounding most of the magnetosphere. However, the Earth's magnetic field drags some particles down through the magnetopause. These particles find their way into the Van Allen radiation belts — a pair of large doughnut-shaped regions in which charged particles are constantly travelling between the Earth's magnetic poles. These charged particles, originating in the solar wind, comprise protons and electrons. The inner Van Allen belt contains mostly protons while electrons form the main content of the outer Van Allen belt.

The inner Van Allen belt is around 1,900 miles (3,000km) thick and reaches to a height of around 3,000 miles (5,000km) above the Earth's surface. The outer Van Allen belt is roughly twice as deep and stretches out to a distance of 12,000 miles (19,000km).

The whole set-up is fairly balanced, until there is an increase in solar sunspot activity. This produces an increase in the number of particles travelling out from the Sun in the solar wind. At these times, the Van Allen belts can become overloaded with some particles spilling out into the upper atmosphere. These particles are travelling at high speeds and they collide with air particles. Reactions are set up in which atoms of oxygen and nitrogen are made to glow. These glows occur at heights of between 65 miles (100km) and 650 miles (1,000km) and produce auroral displays.

Below: *There are two radiation belts around the Earth. They are called the Van Allen belts. The inner belt lies at a distance of about 1.6 Earth radii, and the outer at about 3.5 Earth radii, measured from the Earth's centre. The doughnut-shaped zones trap electrically charged particles. When these particles 'leak' into the upper atmosphere they produce auroral displays.*

Where aurorae may be seen

Aurorae are generally concentrated into the regions above the Earth's north and south magnetic poles and are therefore most often seen from latitudes well away from the equator. Aurorae can have many different shapes including arcs, bands and rays. Although they are usually seen from latitudes well away from the equator, on rare occasions really prominent displays can be spotted from a much wider range.

Aurorae seen in the northern hemisphere are known as the 'aurora borealis' — a name which means 'northern dawn' ('aurora

Below: *The American satellite Explorer 1 discovered the inner Van Allen belt in 1958. Explorer 7 (below) established a link between the radiation belts and activity on the Sun.*

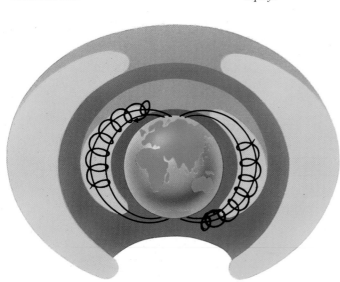

australis' describes those aurorae seen in the southern hemisphere). The reference to dawn is very appropriate. To those observers well away from the main auroral zones, aurorae appear as little more than glows on the northern (or southern) horizons, similar to the glows seen before sunrise. Street lights and other forms of light pollution are bad news for the would-be aurora observer as they can interfere with the display, often rendering it invisible. People who live in cities have little chance of seeing an aurora.

What to watch out for

For many, vivid auroral displays rarely occur and it is always worth keeping an eye on the northern (or southern) horizon for any aurorae that may take place. Telescopes are useless for observing aurorae. They have only relatively narrow fields of view and will show no detail whatsoever. Even binoculars have limited use and are only useful for

determining background stars to enable you to work out the extent of the display.

Aurorae are best observed with the naked eye, which will give you a good overall view of the display and will also leave your hands free to take down any notes you may want to make. These may include written descriptions of what you see together with drawings (which should include the positions of bright background stars).

Make a note of any colour that you see in the display. You can even estimate the brightness of the aurora by comparing it to other celestial objects, such as the Moon or Milky Way, or even to moonlit clouds. Really bright aurorae can even cast shadows! Taking notes of the above details will help you to preserve the memory of any aurora that you may see.

If you would like to make more detailed observations, you should contact one of the national astronomical organisations.

Above: *The aurora borealis is the result of charged particles entering the Earth's upper atmosphere.*

Really strong aurorae may even be seen from city areas, and what at first may be nothing more than a glow on the horizon could grow into huge arcs stretching across the sky. Rays emerging from the arc may give the aurora the appearance of a huge cosmic curtain fluttering in the sky. These ray formations follow the lines of force from the Earth's magnetic field — lines of force which resemble those surrounding an ordinary bar magnet. Unfortunately, vivid displays like this are rare and, unless you happen to live more than 50° or so from the equator, it is unlikely that you will see anything more than an horizon glow or, perhaps, an arc. However, take heart! Bright displays *do* occur; when they do, and if you are fortunate enough to see one, the ethereal, ghostlike display will long be remembered.

THE STARS

BRIGHTNESS AND DISTANCE

As long ago as 150BC, the Greek astronomer Hipparchus divided up the stars into six classes according to their apparent brightness. The first class contained the brightest objects in the sky, and the sixth, the faintest. Today we use the same basic system, although we can now estimate magnitudes to within a margin of 0·01 — unlike the rather crude method of Hipparchus.

Magnitude systems
A star of 1st magnitude is 100 times as bright as one of 6th magnitude. This means that the difference between successive magnitudes is 2·512. In other words, a star of magnitude 2·00 is 2·512 times as bright as one of magnitude 3·00, 6·31 (2·512 x 2·512) times as bright as a star of magnitude 4·00 and so on. The brightest objects in the sky are given negative magnitudes in order that they fit in with the magnitude scale. Sirius, the brightest star, has a magnitude of −1·42, closely followed by Canopus at magnitude −0·72.

Other celestial objects have also had their magnitudes assessed. The Sun has a magnitude of −26·8, and the full Moon an average magnitude of −12·7. Venus, the brightest of the planets, can reach a magnitude of −4·4 while Pluto, on the other hand, has a maximum magnitude of around 14.

The lower the number, the brighter the object, with minus numbers signifying the brightest objects in the sky. The faintest objects photographed so far have magnitudes of around 26. A pair of 7 x 50 binoculars will show stars down to around 9th magnitude, whereas a small telescope will reveal stars a magnitude fainter.

Absolute magnitudes
The above system classifies how bright stars *appear* to the observer. Although the Sun is the brightest object in the sky, it only appears so bright because it is close to us. If it were at the same distance as many of the other stars, it would be very faint indeed. The standard magnitude system is not a proper guide to the *true* luminosity of the star.

To express the *actual* brightness of stars, astronomers use the 'absolute magnitude' system. The absolute magnitude of a star is the apparent magnitude the star *would* have if placed at a standard distance of 32·6 light years or 10 parsecs (see below). If the Sun were placed at this distance, its magnitude would be only +4·83. We therefore say the Sun's absolute magnitude is 4·83.

Parsec
A parsec is the distance at which a star would have a *par*allax of one *sec*ond of arc. This distance amounts to 3·26 light years. Actually, there are no stars this close to the Earth. The closest is Proxima Centauri which has a measured parallax of 0·762 seconds of arc and lies at a distance of 4·34 light years.

Measuring stellar distances
In order to work out how bright a star really is, its distance has to be calculated. There are several ways of doing this. The most straightforward is to measure a star's parallax, or apparent shift, against the background of more distant stars, when viewed from two different positions.

Parallax can be demonstrated by a simple experiment. Simply close one eye and hold up your finger at arm's length, lining it up with a distant object such as a tree. Without moving your finger, look at it through the other eye. Your finger will appear to move in relation to the tree because you are looking at it from a slightly different direction. Knowing the distance between your eyes, and the angle by which your finger appeared to shift enables the distance to your finger to be worked out using simple trigonometry.

When used to work out star distances, trigonometrical parallax entails the measurement of the shift of a nearby star against the background of more distant stars, when viewed from opposite points in the Earth's orbit around the Sun. The principle of trigonometrical parallax had been known for a long time, yet it took several attempts by different astronomers before it was successfully used to determine the distance to a star.

In 1838, the German astronomer Friedrich Wilhelm Bessel used the parallax method to work out the distance to the star 61 Cygni. Bessel's skills as an observer, coupled with his

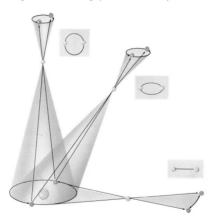

Above: *As we orbit the Sun, the apparent position of a nearby star will change against the background of other stars. If the star is near the pole of the Earth's orbit, the star's path will appear almost circular. It becomes elliptical as the star's inclination decreases. At zero inclination it is a straight line.*

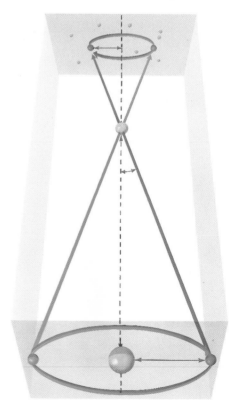

Right: *The parallax method can measure a star's distance. The star's position against the stellar background is observed when the Earth is at one position in its orbit (left) then six months later (right). The apparent change in position gives its parallax. This is one half the angle of the apparent variation.*

The light year

*I*n order to express large distances in space, astronomers use a unit of length known as a 'light year', rather than miles or kilometres. To describe the distances to remote stars in miles would be like expressing the distance across North America in inches, so large and unwieldy would be the numbers! A light year is equal to the distance that a ray of light, travelling at 186,000 miles (300,000km) per second, would traverse in a year. This distance is equivalent to 5,878,000,000,000 miles (9,460,000,000,000km)! In other words, to say the star Vega in Lyra is 27 light years away means that the light we are seeing from the star today set off towards us 27 years ago!

The distances are, in fact, measured from our local star, the Sun. But it is acceptable to say Vega is 27 light years away from us, on Earth. After all, we are only 8.3 light minutes from the Sun.

Right: *The first astronomer to achieve success with the parallax method was Friedrich Bessel. He observed the star 61 Cygni. Cygnus is an easily recognised northern hemisphere constellation (see also star chart on page 57). The five dominant stars form a cross which is the outline for the swan.*

Below: *It is not possible to tell how far away things are by simply looking at them. The yellowish stars are in the distance. Much closer to us are the blue stars. In the same region is a dark cloud blocking out the more distant starlight.*

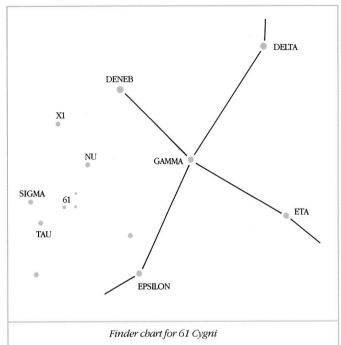

Finder chart for 61 Cygni

access to telescopes and equipment better than those of his predecessors, enabled him to measure 61 Cygni's tiny parallax shift. He calculated the distance of 61 Cygni to be 10·3 light years, close to the presently accepted distance of just over 11 light years.

Trigonometrical parallax can only be used to determine the distance to relatively nearby stars. The further away a star is, the smaller (and more difficult to measure) is its angular shift against the stellar background. Similarly, the further away your finger is from your eye, the smaller is its angular shift against the background, when viewed through each eye alternately. The system can only be used on stars at a distance of around 70 light years. There are about 1,400 stars within 70 light years of the Earth, nearly 1,000 of which have had their distances calculated very accurately.

If a star lies at a distance of more than 70 light years, its distance must be worked out differently. In these cases, astronomers compare a star of known distance with one of the same type, but lying at an unknown distance from us. Assuming that two stars of similar type will have similar luminosities, astronomers can work out the distance to the star furthest away by comparing both its apparent and actual brightnesses. The accuracy of this method hinges on being able to assess a distant star's type and brightness with accuracy.

THE MESSAGE OF STARLIGHT

Stars are so far away that they appear as points of light through even the world's largest telescopes. In order to examine stars in more detail, astronomers must get as much information as possible out of the actual light that is reaching the telescope. Much of our current knowledge of the stars has come to us through the use of the spectroscope.

Stellar spectra

If the light from a star is passed through a prism, it will be split up into a band of constituent colours called a spectrum. A familiar example of this effect is a rainbow. Light is a waveform, with different colours resulting from different wavelengths. As with sound waves, the wavelength is the distance from one wave crest to the next. The electromagnetic spectrum is made up of the complete range of electromagnetic radiation of which visible light forms only a tiny part. It ranges from short-wavelength violet through blue, green, yellow and orange to long-wavelength red. Radiation with wavelengths shorter than visible light include ultraviolet, X-rays and gamma rays. Longer wavelength radiation includes infra-red radiation and radio waves.

High density gases, like those found deep within a star, produce an unbroken sequence of colours. This is called a continuous spectrum. However, low density gas, such as that which is found above the surface of stars, will produce a spectrum in the form of a series of bright individual lines. Each of these lines is the result of the effects of a particular element, present within the gas, producing the spectrum. This is an emission spectrum.

The spectrum of a star contains an emission spectrum superimposed on a continuous spectrum. The lines of the emission spectrum are actually seen as dark bands in contrast with the brighter continuous spectrum underneath. Each line indicates the presence of a particular element within the atmosphere of the star being observed. If the star is moving either towards or away from us, the lines of the emission spectrum are shifted towards either the blue or the red end of the spectrum. In the case of a receding star, the wavelengths of light are stretched a little, producing a shift of the spectral lines towards red, or long-wavelength, end. The lines in the spectrum of an approaching star are shifted towards the blue, or short-

wavelength, end. This effect is known as the 'red (or 'blue') shift' — the amount of shift being an indication of how quickly a star is travelling towards or away from us. The greater the spectral shift, the higher the velocity.

Spectroscopy

The study of stellar spectra is known as spectroscopy. The spectra are produced by an instrument called a spectroscope. This is attached to the telescope and splits the starlight up into its individual wavelengths or colours. In 1863, the Italian astronomer Angelo Secchi published the first classification of stellar spectra. He introduced a classification of four different types of star based on their spectral appearances, although astronomers at the time, did not really understand the significance of the spectral lines.

During the early 1900s, an improved classification was formulated by the American astronomer Annie Jump Cannon and her colleagues at Harvard Observatory. This new classification was called the Harvard classification and it identified stars according

Above: *This photograph of the region surrounding the star Rho Ophiuci was made by combining three black and white images taken through different colour filters. This technique produces greater detail. The bright regions contain young stars, but our view is obscured by dense clouds of dust.*

Right: *The Hertzsprung-Russell diagram is familiar to most astronomers. It relates a star's luminosity (its rate of energy output) to its spectral type (its surface temperature). The diagram represents stellar characteristics. Most stars, including the Sun fall within the band called the Main Sequence–the diagonal band running from top left to bottom right. Another band, above and to the right of the main sequence, is made up of giants. Above the giants are supergiants. At bottom left are stars, like white dwarfs, at the end of their lives.*

Star colours

The colour of a star is a good indication of its surface temperature. The hottest stars, spectral classes O, B and A, are blue-white or white. A typical example is the bright star Spica (B1) in Virgo. Below these we have the yellow stars of spectral classes F and G, including Polaris (F8) and the Sun (G2) followed by the orange K-type stars, of which Dubhe in Ursa Major (K0) is an example. Finally we have the red stars of types M, R, N and S—a well-known example being Betelgeuse in Orion (M2), marking the Hunter's right shoulder.

A number of the brighter stars have colours which are prominent to the naked eye. The ruddy glow of Betelgeuse in Orion is unmistakable. Rigel, also in Orion, is a brilliant blue-white star while Capella in Auriga has a yellowish hue. However, the naked eye can only readily distinguish the colours of the brightest stars, although binoculars and telescopes will reveal many other star colours. Mu Cephei, nicknamed by William Herschel as the Garnet star, is one of the reddest naked-eye stars in the sky. Binoculars will bring out the strong colour of this object very well.

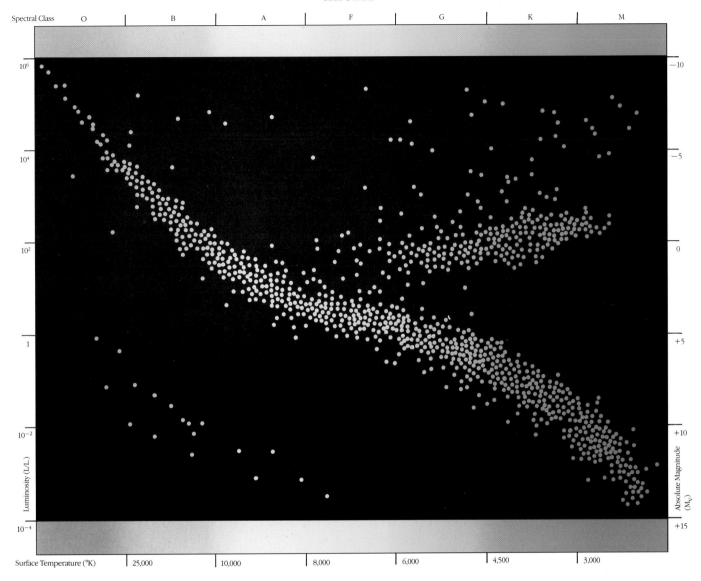

Spectral Class   O   B   A   F   G   K   M

Luminosity (L/L.): 10^6, 10^4, 10^2, 1, 10^{-2}, 10^{-4}

Absolute Magnitude (M_V): −10, −5, 0, +5, +10, +15

Surface Temperature (°K): 25,000   10,000   8,000   6,000   4,500   3,000

to their temperatures. Different spectral classes were designated letters from the sequence O, B, A, F, G, K, M, R, N and S (the last three letters were added later).

The spectral class of a star is a clear indication of its temperature. The hottest stars, with surface temperatures exceeding 63,000°F (35,000°C), are classed as O while the coolest M, R, N and S stars have surface temperatures of around 5,500°F (3,000°C) or less. These broad classifications have been further subdivided by the insertion of a number, ranging from zero to nine, after the letter. For example, the Sun is classed as a G2 star.

The Hertzsprung-Russell diagram

This is a diagrammatic classification of stars which plots their spectral types or temperatures against their absolute magnitude or luminosity. It was drawn up after work by the American astronomer Henry Norris Russell and the Danish Ejnar Hertzsprung in the early 1900s. They were independently considering how a star's spectral type could be related to its brightness. They realised that, when the magnitudes and colours of a number of stars were plotted against each other, a regular pattern emerged. Hertzsprung was the first to note this, followed a few years

later by Russell's discovery of the regularity. Generally speaking, hot stars are seen towards the left-hand side of the diagram with cool stars near the right. Bright stars are found near the top and faint stars near the bottom.

Extending from the upper left to lower right of the diagram is a band of stars that we call the Main Sequence. Stars whose properties place them within this region of the diagram are called Main Sequence stars. Hertzsprung and Russell had noticed that one or two stars were scattered to either side of this band; and subsequent observation revealed the presence of more groups.

STELLAR EVOLUTION

The stars we see today are the same as those seen thousands of years ago. They have changed little between the time that the early star catalogues were drawn up and now. Changes that take place within a star happen over extremely long periods of time, and establishing the full life story of a star — from its original formation inside a nebula through to its final stage as a white dwarf, neutron star or black hole — may seem a difficult task.

However, astronomers overcame this problem by studying large numbers of stars. Each star is at a different stage of its evolution, and by piecing together all the observations, we can work out the 'sequence of events' that takes place.

A star is born

Stars are formed inside vast interstellar clouds of gas and dust by a process known as gravitational collapse. These clouds, or nebulae, comprise mainly hydrogen — the most common element in the universe.

The process of star formation starts when the nebula is disrupted, perhaps by shock waves given off by a nearby supernova explosion or even radiation pressure from nearby young, hot stars. The disruption causes regions of the nebula to collapse in on themselves producing clumps of material.

As the clumps undergo collapse, their densities and internal temperatures increase. As the density grows, it becomes more and more difficult for the heat generated to escape. Eventually, the heat reaches such a high degree that its outward pressure of expansion stops the gravitational collapse. The original nebula now contains a number of hot and relatively dense stable regions. These regions are called protostars.

Stellar birthplaces

The Horsehead Nebula in Orion is a typical example of a dark nebula, and is one of many such objects known to astronomers. Small patches of dark nebulosity are often seen silhouetted against bright nebulosity. A good example is the Rosette Nebula (NGC 2244) in Monoceros. These patches, or Bok Globules, are named after the Dutch/American astronomer Bart Bok who first drew attention to them. Around 200 have been catalogued. Their masses range from a little over that of the Sun to 200 times the mass of the Sun, and their diameters from a

tenth to a couple of light years. Bok Globules are three-quarters hydrogen and one-quarter helium, with traces of other, heavier elements.

The star begins to shine

What happens to the protostar depends on its mass. If this is similar to the Sun, nuclear reactions take place at its core where the temperature reaches 28 million °F (15 million °C). These reactions (nuclear fusion) mean that four hydrogen atoms are crushed together to form one atom of helium. However, the resulting helium atom is lighter than the original four atoms of hydrogen, and a tiny amount of mass is left over from the reaction. This mass escapes to the surface of the star and is given off as light and heat.

Right: *Stars in the main sequence band of the Hertzsprung-Russell diagram convert hydrogen to helium in their cores (1). As the hydrogen is depleted, the core contracts and heats up; hydrogen starts to burn in a shell around it. Further contraction heats the core until helium burning starts. The energy created causes the outer stellar envelope to expand into space, swelling the star in size. Its outer layers cool and glow red; the star is now a Red Giant (2, see scale drawing left). When the helium is exhausted, the core contracts again and grows hotter until nuclear burning of heavier elements formed by helium fusion begins in concentric shells around the core (3). Eventually an inert iron core is formed.*

Right: *Hidden in this dust and gas cloud is a baby star (arrowed). It is so young it does not shine, and was detected by the heat it emits.*

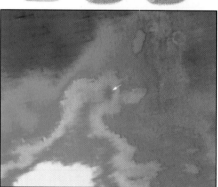

Because the outward force of the heat generated balances the collapse through gravity, the star becomes stable. Stars of mass similar to the Sun contain enough hydrogen 'fuel' for them to shine for around 10,000 million years before further changes happen. The Sun has been shining in this way for 5,000 million years, and will continue to do so for as long again.

Onto the main sequence

The conversion of hydrogen to helium by nuclear fusion takes up the longest phase of a star's life. During this time, the star appears on the Main Sequence of the Hertz-sprung-Russell Diagram (see The Message of Starlight). As we have seen, just how long a star takes to exhaust its hydrogen supply, and

Above: *The Orion Nebula (left) and the Horsehead Nebula (right) are revealed in all their glory by this long-exposure photograph. They are clouds of gas which become prominent either by emitting light (ON) or by obscuring the light from bright nebulae or stars beyond (HN).*

therefore remain on the Main Sequence, depends on its initial mass. Stars with less than one solar mass may have much longer lifetimes; their hydrogen being consumed at a slower rate. More massive stars, however, use up their hydrogen fuel at a much faster rate. As the conversion of hydrogen to helium goes on, the ratio of hydrogen to helium within the star changes. Eventually the hydrogen fuel store runs down, and the star enters the next stage of its life.

From main sequence to planetary nebula

While there is sufficient hydrogen available at the core, helium will continue to be formed. However, the hydrogen fuel will eventually diminish, and the helium production will decrease dramatically. The Sun will reach this stage in around 5,000 million years, at which time its core will already be rich in helium, and the amount of heat energy given off by the core will be reduced. This will upset the state of balance, and the star will have difficulty in supporting its outer layers which will then tend to press downwards with more force through the effects of gravity. The core will become slightly more compressed and get warmer. The hydrogen to helium reaction will carry on in a shell surrounding the core,

and it is here that most of the star's energy is produced. The star remains on the Main Sequence for a few million more years, still shining due to the conversion of hydrogen to helium.

Eventually, all hydrogen fuel in the core is exhausted, and the only hydrogen burning is in the surrounding shell. There is now no heat being produced in the core, and gravity once more tries to take over. The core contracts and heats up, producing heat energy. This helps the star to counterbalance the pull of gravity. However, further nuclear reactions will not take place until the core temperature reaches 180 million °F (100 million °C). The hydrogen burning shell continues to produce helium, which falls onto the core and so increases its mass. This

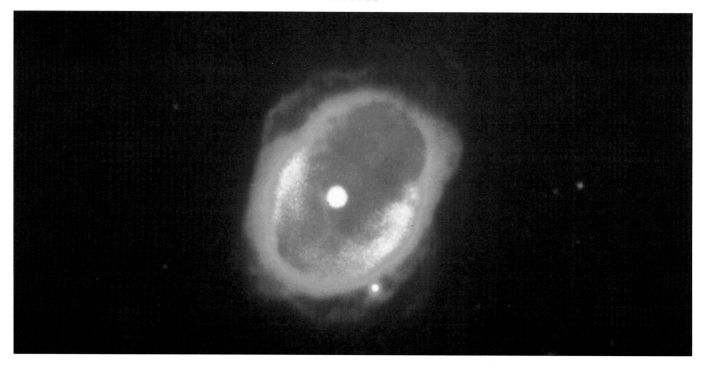

creates an increased inward pull through gravity, so raising the core's temperature.

Red giants

Eventually the core becomes so compressed that it is only a small fraction of its original size. There is a corresponding increase in its internal temperature and pressure which increase its energy output, and force the star's outer layers to expand into surrounding space. The star grows to many times its original size, and its outer layers cool to around 6,330 °F (3,500 °C). The star now glows red and is classed as a 'red giant'. There are many examples of red giants in the sky, notable among which is Aldebaran — the brightest star in Taurus.

Our Sun will turn into a red giant in around 5,000 million years time. As it does so, the inner planets will be consumed and the outer gas giants will have their thick atmospheres vaporised, leaving their rocky cores exposed to space. Although the surface temperature of the Sun will be greatly reduced, it will be much larger than it is now, and its luminosity will be increased by a hundred times.

The outer layers of red giants are very thin and tenuous. However, their cores become highly compressed which causes the temperature to rise. This temperature will eventually reach 180 million °F (100 million °C)

Above: *Planetary nebulae are shells of gas thrown off by a giant star near the end of its life. As the star evolves into a white dwarf it flings off material. A gas shell around the remaining small and very hot white dwarf is formed. The planetary nebula shown above is in the constellation of Vela.*

at which point the helium undergoes its own nuclear reactions and converts into carbon.

Eventually, the helium fuels runs out, and the core once more contracts. As far as low mass stars are concerned, there will be no further nuclear reactions, and the star will slowly contract and slow down, ending up as a 'white dwarf' (see later). Stars with more mass evolve differently from here: the carbon core contracts further and produces more nuclear fusion which enables the star to continue shining.

Planetary nebulae

Before a star cools and becomes a white dwarf, radiation pressure from the core can blow away its outer layers. These will form an expanding shell of gas known as a planetary nebula. The material forming planetary nebulae will eventually be pushed into interstellar space. These small gaseous structures are relatively short-lived with average life-spans of only several tens of thousands of years.

Above right: *The supernova that was seen in our galaxy in 1572 is known as Tycho's Star, after the astronomer Tycho Brahe. Today radio telescopes can detect the expanding shell of material that remains from the explosion. The core of the original star is now a neutron star, it is too faint to be seen.*

White dwarfs

Eventually, the red giant's fuel will become exhausted and no further reactions will take place. The halt of nuclear reactions means that there will be no more outward-acting heat pressure. Gravity then takes over and the star collapses — stars of less than 1.4 times the mass of the Sun collapsing to form white dwarfs. As the tremendous pull of gravity predominates, the atoms from which the star is formed become tightly packed. So severe is the compression that the star is crushed to immense densities. A star similar to our Sun would have a density of up to a million times that of water and be packed into a sphere with a diameter of only a few thousand miles. Compare this with the Sun's present diameter of 865,000 miles (1,392,000 km)!

In spite of the fact that nuclear reactions will have stopped, the star will continue to shine. There will be heat produced during the collapse, although this would eventually completely radiate into surrounding space, leaving a dead star called a black dwarf.

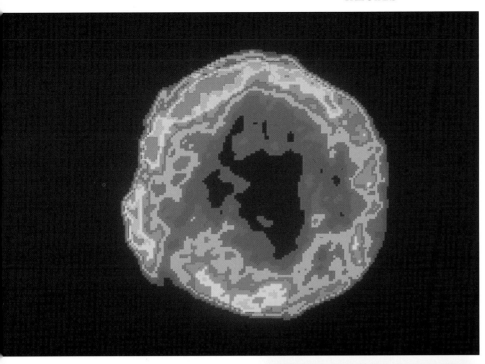

ture climbs at a phenomenal rate. A violent nuclear reaction takes place which blasts the outer layers of the star into surrounding space. For a time the exploding star can even outshine the entire galaxy of which it is a member! The ejection of material is considerably more forceful than that which accompanies the formation of a planetary nebula.

Following the explosion, the core collapses to form a neutron star. The material forming the Crab Nebula is actually the scattered remains of the 1054 supernova; and the pulsar inside the Crab has now been identified as a rapidly spinning neutron star which emits radio pulses at a rate equal to its rotation period. This is around 30 times per second! Several hundred pulsars have now been found, although only a small number have been identified optically.

Black holes

Stars that have masses of more than eight times that of the Sun may suffer a totally irresistible gravitational contraction. This produces a sphere of increasing density and decreasing size. As the density grows, the escape velocity of the star also increases until it eventually exceeds the speed of light. To a nearby observer, the star would simply disappear once light was unable to escape from its surface.

The gravitational pull of the collapsed star lessens with increasing distance. Eventually a point is reached from which light can escape. This is the event horizon. Beneath the event horizon is a spherical volume of space which is forever hidden from view. This zone is a black hole. Black holes represent the final stage in the evolution of very massive stars. We cannot actually see them and little evidence for their existence has been gathered.

Conclusive evidence may eventually come from the study of binary stars. Astronomers can calculate the masses of the stars in binary systems by watching closely their behaviour and orbital motions. Binary systems are often found to contain one very massive star, usually either a white dwarf or neutron star although a number are thought to contain black holes.

One binary system that is a candidate for containing a black hole is the X-ray source Cygnus X-1, the optical companion of which is the supergiant star HDE 226868. Measurements have shown that HDE 226868 has an invisible companion with a mass too great for it to be either a white dwarf or neutron star. The conclusion that some astronomers have drawn is that the unseen star is a black hole.

Neutron stars and pulsars

The collapse of stars with masses of between 1·4 and 3 times that of the Sun takes them beyond the white dwarf stage. The colossal pull of gravity exerted by these stars on themselves is so great that their protons and electrons are smashed together to form neutrons. This gives rise to a neutron star. Neutron stars have such high densities that a tablespoonful of their material would have a mass of around 15 million tons! Neutron stars have diameters of only a few tens of miles.

Before 1967, neutron stars existed only in theory. Observational evidence was gathered in 1967 when bursts of radio emission were detected from an area of sky which contained no visible source. These signals were being transmitted at the rate of one every 1·3370109 seconds. First thoughts were that a pulsating star was giving off the signals. The star was referred to as a 'pulsar'. A search through previous observations revealed three more. Since then, many have been found, notably one at the heart of the Crab Nebula in Taurus.

In 1054, Chinese astronomers recorded the appearance of a new and very bright star in the constellation of Taurus. The object they saw was in fact a supernova—an event which occurs as the result of the gravitational collapse of a very massive star. The collapse is so forceful that the star's internal tempera-

Above: *The Einstein Observatory satellite made this false-colour image of the x-ray source Cygnus X-1. Its name is from Cygnus, the parent constellation, and X-1 because it is the first X-ray source to be found in that constellation. Cygnus X-1 has a partner, a blue supergiant. This star also has a companion which is invisible and we can only estimate its mass. Results suggest that it could be a black hole, but we cannot be certain.*

DOUBLE AND MULTIPLE STARS

Unlike the Sun, which is on its own in space, most of the stars we see are members of multiple star systems. These can be anything from simple binary stars, consisting of a pair of stars orbiting one another, to the sometimes huge open or globular star clusters (see Star Clusters).

What is a double star?

In many cases, the two stars we see forming a double star system are mutually related. They are linked together through their common gravitational attraction. However, there are many cases of stars which only appear to be close to one another in space. These are the so-called *optical doubles* which comprise two (or more) stars which happen to lie in the same line of sight as seen from Earth. In other words, their apparent association is nothing more than a chance alignment. An example is the wide naked-eye pair Alpha[1] and Alpha[2] Capricorni. In reality, Alpha[1] is many times further away than Alpha[2]. At first, most astronomers believed that all double stars were due to chance alignment. However in 1802, William Herschel proved through observation that in many cases the two stars were actually orbiting one another.

Systems in which pairs of stars are orbiting in this way are called 'binary stars' — the two components moving around their common centre of gravity. Their periods of revolution can be anything from less than an hour to many thousands of years. The binary with the shortest known orbital period is the X-ray star X-1820-303 in the globular cluster NGC 6624. Lying at a distance of almost 30,000 light years, the X-1820-303 system comprises two stars which orbit one another once every 11min 25sec!

It is difficult to measure the orbital periods of binaries whose stars are situated a long way apart, as these periods may amount to many millions of years. Such is the case with Epsilon Lyrae — the famous 'double-double' star in Lyra. Observers with very keen eyesight will see that Epsilon Lyrae, located close to the brilliant star Vega, is a double, although a telescope will reveal that each of the two main components is double again. These two doubles are actually binary systems whose components orbit one another every 1,165 years in the case of Epsilon[1], and 585 years in the case of Epsilon[2]. However, it is also thought that the Epsilon[1] and Epsilon[2] systems orbit each other over a period of around a million years.

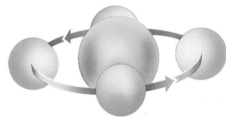

Above: *As the two stars in a binary system revolve around each other one may partly or wholly eclipse the other. This depends on the view of the stars' orbit from Earth. In an eclipsing binary the two stars are orbiting in a* plane which is on or very close to the line of sight from Earth. These double stars are detected by the periodic variation in the brightness of the stars, such as Algol. Here one star is much brighter than the other.

Spectroscopic binaries

Although the components of binary systems are often visible through telescopes, sometimes the stars are so closely situated that even the world's largest telescopes are unable to show both components. These objects can only be identified by using a spectroscope (see The Message of Starlight). The spectrum of a very close binary system will be a combination of the spectra of two stars.

If the plane of orbit of the two stars in a binary system is lined up with Earth, there will be times when one component is approaching us and the other moving away (see The Message of Starlight). If a star is moving towards us, the light waves coming from it will be squashed up, thereby making them shorter. If the star is moving away, they will be stretched out, becoming longer. This effect is known as the 'blue shift' (or 'red shift') — the

Left: *Epsilon Lyrae is a double double star. It is shown here, in the top left of this night sky view. The bright star Vega is in the centre of the picture. This is the view you can expect to see with binoculars. The two stars visible in Epsilon are magnitude 4.7 and 5.1. A more powerful instrument will show that they are both double stars.*

Right: *For northern hemisphere observers Ursa Major contains an interesting double star. It is one of the seven bright stars in the tail and back of the bear, known as the Plough. It is Mizar, the brightest star in this picture. Its companion is Alcor, shown to its lower left. These two are an optical pair. But Mizar is itself a double, and each of its components are spectroscopic binaries. Alcor is also a spectroscopic binary. So the original star turns out to be a multiple with six components.*

amount of shift being an indication of how quickly a star is travelling towards or away from us. The greater the spectral shift, the higher the velocity.

A similar effect is noticed with sound waves. The sound waves from the siren of an approaching fire engine will be compressed. This makes the wavelength shorter, and therefore the note will be higher. Once the fire engine passes, however, the sound waves are stretched out, and the note is lower. The greater the difference in the two notes emitted by the siren, the greater the velocity of the fire engine as its passes.

The lines of the emission spectrum of the approaching star will be shifted towards the blue end of the spectrum while those of the receding star will be shifted in the opposite direction. In other words, the spectral lines will become separated into a sort of 'concer-

tina effect'. When the two stars are moving across our line of sight, there will be no shift, and the spectral lines will appear single.

In around 1650, the Italian astronomer Giovanni Riccioli discovered an optical companion to Mizar (the star at the centre of the Plough 'handle') thus making it the first double to be discovered with a telescope. The positions of the two stars (Mizar A and Mizar B) relative to one another has changed since discovery, although the change is only very slight, which indicates an orbital period of many thousands of years.

In 1889, the American astronomer Edward Charles Pickering noticed that the lines in the spectrum of Mizar A occasionally became doubled. He concluded (correctly) that Mizar A has a companion which is too close to be resolvable with a telescope, making Mizar A the first binary to be detected spectroscopic-

ally. Mizar B is now also known to be a spectroscopic binary, making Mizar a quadruple star system. Alcor, the naked-eye companion of Mizar, is also a spectroscopic binary. Alcor and Mizar are around a quarter of a light year apart.

Multiple star systems

There are many other examples of multiple star systems, including the triple star Alpha Centauri. The two main components orbit one another every 79·9 years and form one of the finest visual binary systems in the sky. The Alpha Centauri system is accompanied by the 10th magnitude red dwarf Proxima Centauri, lying about a sixth of a light year from its brighter companions. Proxima Centauri is a little closer to us and is actually the closest star to the Sun. It is thought that Proxima orbits the main Alpha Centauri pair over a period of around half a million years.

VARIABLE STARS

Although most stars shine steadily, some show variations in brightness. These so-called variable stars are split into two main groups: *extrinsic* and *intrinsic* variables. Extrinsic variables change in brightness through the effects of another object, and intrinsic variables because of changes occurring within the star itself. These two basic classes are divided into many different individual types, details of some of which are given below.

Extrinsic variables: eclipsing binaries

The most numerous type of extrinsic variable is the eclipsing binary. Eclipsing binary systems contain two stars orbiting their common centre of gravity. Because the plane of their orbit is in line with Earth, the stars alternately hide (or eclipse) one another. These eclipses produce reductions in the overall light output of the system as the light (or part of the light) from the hidden star is blocked off.

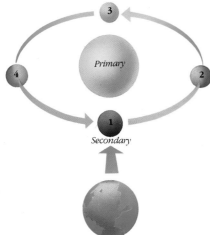

Above: *In the eclipsing binary Algol, one star is much brighter than the other. The diminution in brightness is most obvious when the faint star eclipses the brighter (1). The light curve, right, shows how the magnitude of the star changes as its companion moves around it.*

Above: *A nova, also known as a guest star, is a special kind of variable star. It flares up dramatically over a few hours and then returns to its original state. In 1976 Nova Vulpeculae flared up to almost magnitude 6. It then faded back into relative obscurity.*

Intrinsic variables: the Cepheids

There are a large number of intrinsic variables all of which vary due to changes taking place within the stars themselves. By far the most famous type is the Cepheid, named after Delta Cephei — the first star of this type to be discovered. Cepheids are short-period, pulsating variables which are very luminous. They can be seen over immense distances. There are well over 500 Cepheids known to astronomers, all of which have periods of between 1 and 55 days. The period of Delta Cephei is 5·37 days during which time it varies between 3rd and 4th magnitudes.

The period-luminosity relationship

There is a definite link between the *actual luminosity* and *periods* of Cepheid variables

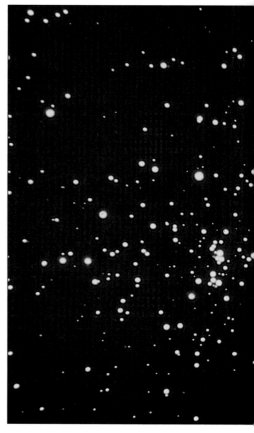

Above: *These two star clusters are the 'Sword Handle' clusters in Perseus. Together they contain around 5,000 times more material than that of our Sun. The one seen on the left is some 8,000 light years away, and the second one is 7,000 light years away.*

— a relationship discovered by the American astronomer Henrietta Swan Leavitt in 1912. A keen observer of variable stars, Henrietta Leavitt was looking at Cepheid variables in the Small Magellanic Cloud (see Beyond The Milky Way) when she noticed that those Cepheids with *longer* periods were always *brighter* than those with shorter periods. Because all the Cepheids observed were at roughly the same distance from us, she decided that those with longer periods were actually more powerful.

This relationship applies to all Cepheids, whether they are in our own Galaxy or other galaxies. It means that the distance to a Cepheid can be worked out by measuring the variations. Once the *actual* brightness has been determined, it is compared to its

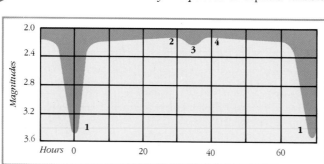

apparent brightness. From this comparison the distance to the star can be worked out. This has greatly helped astronomers to determine how far away galaxies are. It was due to the study of Cepheids in the Andromeda Spiral Galaxy that the American astronomer Edwin Hubble was able to prove that galaxies were systems far beyond the boundaries of our own Milky Way Galaxy.

Long-period variables

The brightest and most famous long-period variable is Mira. As with other long-period variables, the maxima and minima of Mira are not constant. Mira fluctuates between 3rd, 4th and 9th magnitude or less. However, on rare occasions it has been known to reach 2nd, or even 1st magnitude. The period is around 331 days but, like the range of brightness, this is subject to change from one cycle to the next.

Long-period variables are very common; around 4,000 are known. They are all red giants (see Stellar Evolution), are subject to large changes in luminosity and have periods of between 200 and 400 days.

Eruptive variables

Eruptive variables include nova-type stars — hot stars which increase in luminosity over short periods before fading back to normal. The decrease in brightness may take years. Of the many observed novae, Nova Aquilae of 1918 was particularly notable. When discovered, Nova Aquilae was at 1st magnitude; yet within only a few hours it was nearly as bright as Sirius! Photographs taken prior to discovery showed that Nova Aquilae had been an 11th magnitude star which had risen to its maximum brightness in just six days. The decrease in brightness took much longer. Nova Aquilae could still be glimpsed with the naked eye nine months later!

Recurrent novae are stars which brighten on more than one occasion, although the increases in brightness are less than those of the 'ordinary' novae. They also fade at a more rapid rate. The brightest and best known example of a recurrent nova is T Coronae Borealis, also known as the 'Blaze Star'.

Novae are members of close binary systems in which one member is usually a white dwarf (see Stellar Evolution). The strong gravity of the white dwarf pulls material away from the larger, cooler companion. This material builds up on the surface of the white dwarf, until the temperature and pressure at the base of the recently deposited layer are high enough to spark off a nuclear reaction. The material is then thrown off into space producing the temporary increase in brightness which we call a nova.

Observing variable stars

Lots of variable stars can be observed with little or no optical aid. Although specialised observation is made both by professional and advanced amateur astronomers, the back-yard star-gazer can have a lot of fun observing variable stars.

Some variables are more suited to beginners than others. Long-period variables are ideal, many of which range from prominent naked-eye visibility down to quite low magnitudes. They need nothing more than binoculars or a small telescope to show their complete cycles of variability. The regular and predictable behaviour of both Cepheids and eclipsing binaries make them ideal targets.

Observing variables: getting started

Those wanting to observe variable stars are advised to join a local astronomical organisation. Many of them have special variable star sections where guidance and encouragement are given. They can provide predictions for a great number of variables, highlighting when different variables will be putting on their changes!

Once a variable star has been selected, actual observation is carried out with the help of what is called a comparison chart. This chart will show the area of sky around the variable and will include not only the variable itself (usually represented by a small circle with a dot at the centre) but other stars of known (and steady) magnitude in the same area of sky. These are the comparison stars — their magnitudes are given either on the chart itself, or on a separate list.

The basic idea behind variable star observation is to compare the brightness of the variable throughout its complete cycle to the nearby stars of known (and steady) magnitude. Although this may sound a clumsy way of making astronomical observations, the practised amateur can learn to estimate stellar magnitudes to quite a high degree of accuracy. Because the star is variable, there will be times when it will be brighter than, as bright as, or fainter than, other comparison stars.

STAR CLUSTERS

Most of the stars that we see in the sky are scattered randomly throughout space, although quite a few are members of small, compact groups. These groups are known as star clusters and there are some which can be seen without optical aid. The most famous examples are the Hyades and Pleiades star clusters in Taurus and the Jewel Box cluster in Crux. Many more can be seen through binoculars, and telescopes show huge numbers. There are two main types of star cluster: open and globular

Open clusters

Open clusters are usually made up of young, hot stars, similar to those found in the spiral arms of our Galaxy, which is where open clusters are generally located. Because of this they are often referred to as *galactic* clusters. They contain anything from a dozen up to many hundreds of stars and are irregular in shape. Diameters of open clusters can be as much as several tens of light years.

Astronomers have identified over a thousand open clusters, many of which are fairly bright and easy to see with the naked eye or through binoculars or a small telescope. The Pleiades is one of the closest, shining from a distance of just over 400 light years. The 500 or so stars in the Pleiades cluster are all fairly young with an age of about 20 million years. Photographs taken through large telescopes show wisps of gas and dust surrounding the stars in the Pleiades. This material is all that is left of the original nebula from which the stars in the Pleiades were formed. The stars forming many other open clusters are also seen to be interlaced with nebulosity.

Another name for the Pleiades cluster is the Seven Sisters which derives from the fact that a person with average eyesight can usually count six or seven individual stars without optical aid. Under excellent sky conditions, however, observers with keen eyesight can see many more. The wide fields of view given by binoculars or a rich field telescope are required to bring out the cluster to best effect since it is spread over such a large area of sky (around the size of the full Moon).

Closer still than the Pleiades is the Hyades open cluster, a gathering of around 400 stars located a little way to the south-east of the

Above: *Two open star clusters, both in the constellation of Taurus, are shown together in this view. On the left is the 'V' shape of the Hyades. Above and to the right, is the Pleiades.*

Left and right: *Use the bright star Deneb to find the star cluster M39. Deneb is the brightest star in Cygnus, and marks the swan's tail. Around 9° away is M39. A semi circle of stars link the two. Binoculars will reveal some of its thirty or so stars.*

Believed to be nearly 14 billion years old (almost three times the age of the Solar System), NGC 188 shines from a distance of 5,000 light years. The stars found in NGC 188 are more like those found in globular clusters (see below). Another peculiarity of NGC 188 is the fact that it lies almost 2,000 light years above the main plane of the Galaxy.

Globular clusters

As their name suggests, globular clusters are huge, spherical collections of stars. Around 200 are known and their diameters can be anything up to several hundred light years. Globulars are among the oldest known type of celestial object, typical globulars containing many tens of thousands of stars and little or none of the nebulosity seen in open clusters. Also, the stars in globulars are quite old, and are similar to those stars found in the central regions of the galaxies. They are tightly packed which allows the strong gravitational attraction between the stars in globulars to preserve the spherical shape of the cluster.

Open clusters are found within the spiral arms of the Galaxy and orbit the centre of the Galaxy in almost circular paths. On the other hand, globular clusters are found in a region known as the galactic halo (see pages 50-51), a spherical volume of space surrounding the Galaxy. Globular clusters orbit the galactic centre in paths that are highly eccentric and greatly tilted with respect to the main plane of the Galaxy.

Of the few globulars that are visible to the naked eye, the brightest is Omega Centauri, a 350 light-year-diameter cluster which is considered by many astronomers to be the best example of a globular cluster in the heavens. Omega Centauri lies at a distance of 17,000 light years and was first mentioned by the Greek astronomer Ptolemy around 2,000 years ago. To the naked eye, Omega Centauri appears as a fuzzy 4th magnitude star; indeed the German astronomer Johann Bayer listed it as a star in his catalogue published in 1603. The first astronomer to observe it as a cluster was the Englishman Edmond Halley in 1677.

Omega Centauri can only be seen satisfactorily from latitudes south of the United States because of its position in the southern sky. For observers further to the north, the Great Globular Cluster (M1) in Hercules is the best example of a naked-eye globular. On really clear nights, M13 can just be glimpsed with the naked eye as a small, spherical patch of light. Located at a distance of slightly over 20,000 light years, this object has a diameter of around 160 light years.

Clusters in other galaxies

*B*oth open and globular clusters have been observed in and around other galaxies. Open clusters are plainly visible in both the Large and Small Magellanic Clouds and the Triangulum Spiral (M33). Among the galaxies seen to be accompanied by globular clusters are the Sombrero Hat Galaxy (M104) in Virgo and the Andromeda Spiral (M31). Approximately 200 globulars have been detected around M31; their distances ranging out to around 100,000 light years from the nucleus.

Above: *Omega Centauri is the brightest globular cluster in the sky. At around 16,000 light years, it is relatively close to Earth and is clearly visible to the naked eye.*

Pleiades, and lying at a distance of about 145 light years. As is often the case with open clusters, many of the stars in the Hyades are considerably fainter than the Sun, and would be difficult or impossible to see if it was much further away. The closeness of the Hyades to the Earth allows astronomers to study typical stars that form open clusters.

The Hyades cluster is thought to be around 400 million years old, far older than the Pleiades. However, this is nowhere near as old as the open cluster NGC 188 in Cepheus.

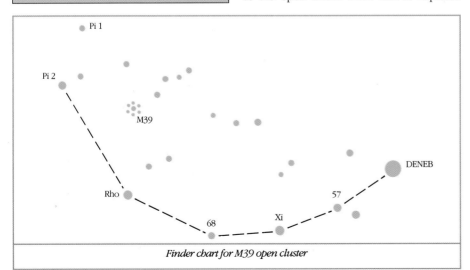

Finder chart for M39 open cluster

NEBULAE

Nebulae are huge interstellar clouds of gas and dust (the name is actually taken from the Latin word *nebula* meaning mist, cloud or vapour). These clouds are concentrations of the huge amounts of gas and dust scattered throughout the spiral arms of the Galaxy. They can appear either as bright, luminous regions or as dark patches superimposed on a brighter background. Some nebulae can be seen with the naked eye, although most lie only within the light grasp of telescopes or binoculars. There are three main types of nebula: emission, reflection and dark.

Emission nebulae

Emission nebulae contain young, hot stars. These stars give off large amounts of ultraviolet radiation which react with the gas in the surrounding nebula, causing it to shine at visible wavelengths. In other words, emission nebulae *emit* their own light.

One of the most famous examples of an emission nebula is the Orion Nebula (M42), visible as a shimmering patch of light a little way to the south of the three stars forming the Belt of Orion. The gas in the Orion Nebula shines through its reaction with the huge amounts of ultraviolet energy given off by the multiple star Theta Orionis, which is buried deep within the cloud.

The Rosette Nebula in Monoceros is another example. Embedded within the Rosette is the large open star cluster NGC 2244, the energy from which causes the nebula to shine. The Rosette is a huge 55 light-year-diameter structure, the light from which has taken over 2,500 years to reach us. Star formation is actually taking place in the Rosette Nebula. Astronomers have observed a number of small, dark, spherical spots known as 'globules'. These are thought to be new stars in the process of formation as the material within the globule slowly collapes under the influence of gravity. Our own Solar System (see pages 10-11) is thought to have condensed from such an object, so these

globules may be scenes of formation of new planetary systems like our own.

Reflection nebulae

As their name suggests, reflection nebulae shine because they *reflect* the light from stars. The stars that exist in and around reflection nebulae are not hot enough actually to cause the surrounding material to give off its own light. Instead, the dust particles within them simply reflect the light from these stars. As a result, reflection nebulae are not as visually impressive as emission nebulae.

The stars in the Pleiades star cluster Taurus are surrounded by reflection nebulosity. Photographs of the Pleiades show the nebulosity as a blue haze, this being the characteristic colour of reflection nebulae, that of emission nebulae being red. The cloud of material surrounding the Pleiades is all that remains of the original cloud from which the stars in the cluster were formed.

Dark nebulae

Situated immediately to the south of the open

star cluster NGC 2264 in Monoceros, is a vast pinnacle of dark matter stretching up into the nebulosity in which the stars of the cluster are embedded. This visually stunning object is the Cone Nebula, and photographs show it to be silhouetted against the brighter background.

As with other dark nebulae, the Cone Nebula appears as a dark patch seen against a brighter background of stars or nebulosity. Dark nebulae contain no stars and simply blot out the light from objects beyond. Another famous example is the Coal Sack in the southern constellation Crux. The Coal Sack was first noted by Portuguese sailors in the 16th century as a huge blot of matter obscuring the star clouds of the southern Milky Way. Lying at a distance of around 500 light years, the Coal Sack has a diameter of over 60 light years.

Planetary nebulae

Planetary nebulae are formed as stars eject their outer layers into surrounding space prior to collapsing to form white dwarfs (see Stellar Evolution). They are seen as shells of gas surrounding the star whose newly exposed surface is typically very hot. Planetary nebulae have nothing whatsoever to do with planets and get their name from the fact that, seen through a telescope, they look like luminous discs, resembling gaseous planets such as Uranus or Neptune.

Finder chart for M57

Beta

Gamma

M57

Above: *The closest planetary nebula to us on Earth is the Helix Nebula. It is in the constellation of Aquarius.*

Left: *The Orion Nebula marks the sword of the hunter Orion. It is an enormous cloud of gas and dust 30 light years in diameter. It appears as a cloudy patch to the naked eye. But powerful telescopes will reveal the star Theta Orionis towards its centre to be four stars, known as the Trapezium.*

Right: *The Ring Nebula in the constellation of Lyra is a planetary nebula. Its spherical shell of glowing gas surrounds a hot central star. The gas shell is continuously expanding. Eventually the gas will be too dispersed to be seen. About a thousand examples of planetary nebulae are known. Use the chart, above right, to find the Ring Nebula, M57, located between the two bright stars in Lyra, Gamma and Beta.*

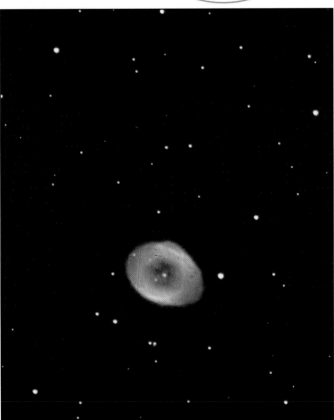

Hundreds of planetary nebulae are known and their ranks include many famous examples, including the Ring Nebula (M57) in Lyra. The Ring Nebula was first seen by the French astronomer Antoine Darquier in 1779, who described it as a dullish disc of light. The star at the centre of the Ring Nebula has a surface temperature of around 180,000°F (100,000°C). This star gives off the huge amounts of ultraviolet energy which cause the gases in the surrounding nebula to shine.

Supernova remnants

The death throes of very massive stars produce another type of nebula. These colossal explosions, known as supernovae (see Stellar Evolution), result in the outer layers of the dying star being thrown off. While the stellar remnant collapses to form either a neutron star or a black hole, the gas cloud expands into surrounding space.

A famous example is the Crab Nebula (M1) in Taurus, an irregularly shaped cloud of material which was formed during the supernova explosion observed by Chinese and Arabic astronomers in 1054. Telescopes reveal an elongated, luminous patch of light just to the north-west of the star Zeta Tauri. Modern observations show that the material within the Crab Nebula is still expanding away from the point at which the original explosion took place and at which a rapidly spinning neutron star has been detected.

THE MILKY WAY GALAXY

The Milky Way Galaxy is a huge, spiral-shaped system. Measuring some 100,000 light years across, it is home to around 100,000 million stars, including the Sun. As well as huge numbers of stars, the Galaxy contains vast amounts of interstellar gas and dust spread throughout the spiral arms of the Galaxy. It is within concentrations of this material (nebulae) that stars continually form.

Although our Galaxy is large, there are many other galaxies that are much bigger, notably the Andromeda Spiral, another member of the Local Group of Galaxies (see Beyond The Milky Way). Also, even though there are millions of other galaxies throughout the universe, the term 'Galaxy' (or 'Milky Way Galaxy') is applied only to our own system.

Our view of the Galaxy

On a clear, dark night we can see a faint, misty band of light crossing the sky. This is the Milky Way and is the view we have as we look out along the main plane of the Galaxy. One of the earliest scientific accounts of the Milky Way was written by the Greek astronomer Ptolemy in about AD150. He described it as 'a zone, which is everywhere as white as milk … neither equal nor regular anywhere, but varies as much in width as in shade or colour … also in some places it is divided into two branches, as is easy to see if we examine it with a little attention'. We can imagine Ptolemy gazing up at the Milky Way and turning his mind to the problem of its form and what it was actually made from.

The divisions and irregularities described by Ptolemy are apparent, the dense starfields of Sagittarius contrasting with the much fainter regions of Monoceros. The Milky Way is brightest in the regions of Cygnus and Aquila in the northern hemisphere and Scorpius and Sagittarius in the southern hemisphere. The width of the Milky Way also varies quite considerably.

Divisions in the Milky Way are visible in the southern constellation Vela, near the bright star Canopus, and from Cygnus to Aquila in the northern sky. The Cygnus-Aquila division is often referred to as the Great Rift. By far the most prominent 'gap' can be found in the southern constellation Crux. This is the Coal Sack—a huge dark cloud of obscuring matter which blots out the light from the stars beyond and gives the appearance of an immense hole in the sky. All these divisions in the Milky Way are due to the presence of dark

Above: *The centre of our Galaxy lies in the constellation of Sagittarius, above left, but clouds of interstellar dust and gas hide our view.*

nebulosity located between us and the starfields beyond.

The idea that the Milky Way is made up of stars was first suggested around 2,000 years ago. Confirmation was provided by Galileo who observed the Milky Way through his small telescopes in the early 17th century. Although the Milky Way teems with stars that appear to be huddled together, in reality they are light years apart. The band of light we see is created by the view of many stars in more or less the same line of sight. Today we can

easily check Galileo's observations either with binoculars or a small telescope.

The galactic disc

The Galaxy has three main regions. These are the central bulge, the disc and the galactic halo. Our Sun lies in the disc between two of the spiral arms that radiate from the central bulge and at a distance of roughly 30,000 light years from the galactic centre, approximately two-thirds of the way out.

The galactic disc has a thickness of around 3,000 light years, although this varies across its width. The stars in the disc travel around the centre of the Galaxy in almost circular orbits — those closer to the centre having

Above: *From Earth our Galaxy looks like a band of stars around the sky. It is this milky river of light that gave it its name. It is shown here crossing Cygnus.*

Right: *This map of the Milky Way contains 7,000 accurately positioned stars. The Magellanic Clouds, companion galaxies to our own are lower right.*

shorter orbital periods than those further out. The Sun takes roughly 225 million years (a 'cosmic year') to travel once around the Galaxy.

The central bulge

The spiral arms contain stars that are generally much younger than those found in the central bulge, where there is little interstellar material compared with the copious amounts scattered throughout the spiral arms. The central bulge is around 10,000 light years thick and has a diameter of around 20,000 light years.

The centre of the Galaxy is located in the constellation Sagittarius, although the gas and dust scattered along the main plane of the Galaxy prevents us from seeing down into the central regions.

However, it is certainly possible to make observations with the use of radio and infra-red telescopes, and astronomers have been able to map the structure of the galactic centre at these wavelengths.

The galactic halo

This is a huge, spherical gathering of stars which completely surrounds the central bulge. The halo contains old stars, like the central bulge, most of which are concentrated into globular clusters which orbit the galactic centre in elliptical paths.

Heavenly walkways

Stretching right around the sky, the Milky Way has figured prominently in legends and mythology which have come down to us from many ancient civilisations. The Romans knew it as the Milky Path, the Hebrews identified it as the River of Light, and the Norsemen thought it was the Path of the Ghosts going to Valhalla — the palace of their heroes killed in battle.

BEYOND THE MILKY WAY

Our Galaxy is one of millions of galaxies that populate the universe. Wherever we look into deep space, beyond the boundary of our own stellar system, huge numbers of glowing shapes can be seen with diameters ranging from several thousand to a hundred thousand light years or more. Although a few are visible without optical aid, large telescopes reveal millions of galaxies, each one of which is home to thousands of millions of stars.

Types of galaxy

Galaxies are classified according to a system devised by the American astronomer Edwin Hubble. Hubble divided galaxies into three basic types: elliptical, spiral and barred spiral. The Milky Way is a spiral with spiral arms radiating from a central bulge. Barred spirals have a bar across their centres from the ends of which spiral arms emerge. Unlike spirals, ellipticals have no spiral formation and are uniform in appearance. They can vary in shape from being almost spherical to highly elongated.

Spiral and barred spiral galaxies are further divided according to the size of their central bulge, and how loosely or tightly wound the

Above: *Galaxies are grouped into clusters. They can contain a handful to a few thousand members, and more than one galaxy type. The Klemola 44 cluster contains many ellipticals and some spirals.*

NGC 3115

NGC 7332

NGC 4762

NGC 4594

NGC 4565

NGC 5907

NGC 4274

NGC 4622

NGC 628

Left: *Galaxies are classified according to their shape. Ellipticals are given the letter E, spirals S, and barred spirals SB. The ones in the top row are all classified as SO. They have a central nucleus and the start of a disc; they are between ellipticals and spirals. These three are not forming stars at present. The other six galaxies are all active star forming systems. They are viewed edge on in the middle row and almost straight on in the bottom row. The bright knots in the spiral arms are regions of newly formed stars. Each galaxy is identified by its NGC number, as listed in the New General Catalogue.*

spiral arms are. There are also a further two classes of galaxy. Irregular galaxies, as their name suggests, are nothing more than loose collections of stars with no definite shape. Lenticular galaxies have a central disc but display little or no evidence of spiral arms. Although irregular and lenticular galaxies were not in the original Hubble classification, they are included today.

The formation of galaxies

Galaxies were formed from regions of material that existed shortly after the Big Bang, although spirals and ellipticals evolved differently. Elliptical galaxies formed quickly with all the material used to make stars. The central regions of spiral galaxies seem to have formed in much the same way. The material left over developed into a disc around the newly formed central regions. As the disc rotated around the centre of the galaxy, shock waves and density waves were produced within the disc material. These waves triggered off regions of collapse within the disc leading to star formation. The stars in the discs of galaxies illuminate the vast clouds of gas and dust in the arms. Stars and interstellar material do exist between the spiral arms, although they are too faint to be readily visible.

Radio galaxies

Although many galaxies give off radio emissions, mainly from their interstellar clouds of gas and dust, some galaxies are very strong radio emitters. The radio energy from normal galaxies comes from visible regions; although there is a class of galaxy from which radio emissions have been detected from well beyond the optically visible regions. Most radio galaxies are elliptical and have radio outputs equivalent to many times that of a normal galaxy. These emissions come from huge radio 'lobes' that stretch far beyond the visible part of the galaxies.

Seyfert galaxies

Seyfert galaxies have weak spiral arms and a small nucleus, the latter being bright and almost starlike in appearance. Seyfert galaxies are named after their discoverer, the American astronomer Carl Seyfert, and emit a great deal of infra-red and ultraviolet energy. They also give out some radio energy and, in some cases, are strong X-ray sources.

The compact spiral galaxy M77 (NGC 1068) in Cetus is a typical Seyfert galaxy. As with other Seyfert galaxies, M77 has colossal gas clouds moving at tremendous speeds in its central regions. These are thought to have been thrown out from the galaxy's nucleus. The velocity of these clouds may be due to the gravitational effects of a massive object at the centre of the galaxy. It has been suggested that black holes (see Stellar Evolution) may be responsible both for the velocity of the gas clouds and the huge amounts of energy given off by Seyfert galaxies.

Groups, clusters and superclusters

Most galaxies are members of groups or clusters. Our own Local Group is a collection of around two dozen galaxies. One of the nearest groups of galaxies to our own is the Ursa Major-Camelopardalis Group; the dozen or so members of this are concentrated around the magnificent spiral galaxy M81 and the unusually shaped M82. Around 50 groups of galaxies lie within a radius of 50 million light years of the Local Group.

Even larger are the clusters, which can contain thousands of galaxies. The nearest rich cluster of galaxies is the Virgo Cluster,

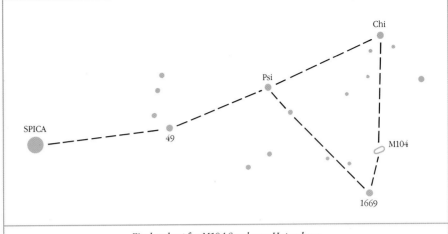

Finder chart for M104 Sombrero Hat galaxy

Left: *The Sombrero Galaxy is a spiral galaxy in Virgo. We see it edge on. Its huge central bulge is very obvious. The resultant sombrero-hat shape gave it its name. The chart, above, will help you locate it. Start by finding the bright star Spica.*

located at a distance of between 40 and 70 million light years. Around 2,000 galaxies have been photographed in the Virgo Cluster. Assuming that dwarf galaxies are also predominant within the Virgo Cluster, as they are in the Local Group, then the total membership may be considerably higher, these fainter galaxies being too dim to be detectable from this distance.

The Virgo Cluster lies at the centre of a huge collection of galaxies known as the Local Supercluster, the diameter of which is in the region of 100 million light years. Member systems include many individual groups of galaxies — our own Local Group being situated near its edge.

The Local Supercluster also includes some solitary galaxies situated in the space between the main groups. Dozens of other super-clusters have been found, each of which contains many smaller clusters scattered across regions of space tens of millions of light years across.

Star Charts

When you first look at the night sky it is difficult to believe that you will soon know your way around it. The sky can look confusing with hundreds of pinpoints of light, and all looking the same. But by taking the sky an area at a time, you will build up your knowledge and observational technique very quickly. These star maps will help you make a start.

Northern hemisphere observers can begin by looking at the constellations centred on the north celestial pole but also the tip of the tail of the little bear, Ursa Minor. The seven dominant stars of Ursa Major are close by. Together they make up the plough, one of the easiest to see of all the star groupings in the sky. On the opposite side of Polaris is Cassiopeia. It has the distinctive shape of a 'W' or an 'M' depending on its position in the sky. These and other constellations can be used as starting points for different tours around the sky.

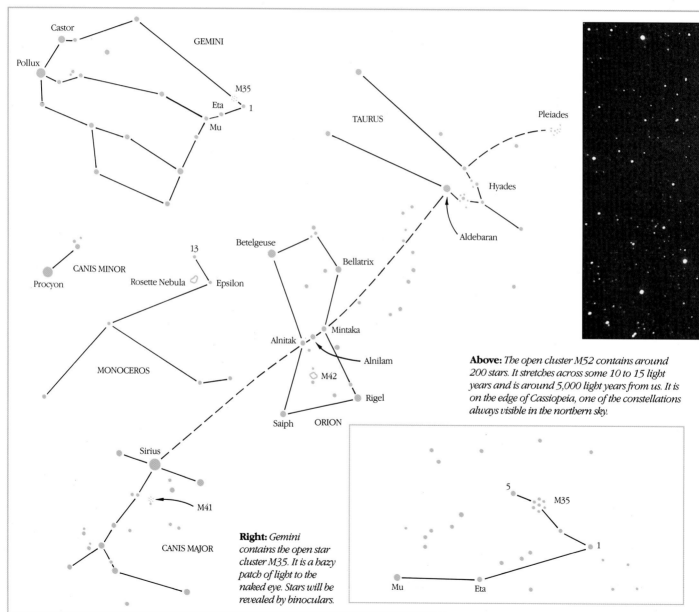

Above: *The open cluster M52 contains around 200 stars. It stretches across some 10 to 15 light years and is around 5,000 light years from us. It is on the edge of Cassiopeia, one of the constellations always visible in the northern sky.*

Right: *Gemini contains the open star cluster M35. It is a hazy patch of light to the naked eye. Stars will be revealed by binoculars.*

A group of easy to see constellations is centred on Orion: they are visible to more stargazers, because they can be seen by northern and southern observers depending on the time of year. The three stars that mark Orion's belt point to Canis Major in one direction and Taurus in the other. Sirius is the brightest star in the whole sky and will be very easy to see. Notice the red colouring of Betelgeuse and the blue-white of Rigel, prominent stars in Orion.

Once you are familiar with the star patterns and know your way round some of the sky, you can move on to the astronomical objects within the constellations. The star fields featured here provide double stars, clusters, and nebulae. These and other examples have been mentioned throughout the book. To find out more about them turn to pages 42-49 and this information, together with the star charts, will help to guide you around the night sky.

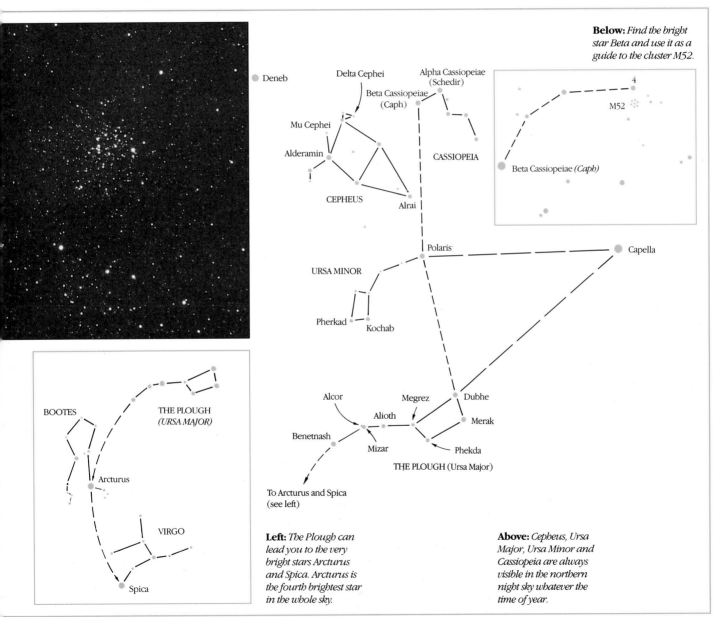

Below: *Find the bright star Beta and use it as a guide to the cluster M52.*

Left: *The Plough can lead you to the very bright stars Arcturus and Spica. Arcturus is the fourth brightest star in the whole sky.*

Above: *Cepheus, Ursa Major, Ursa Minor and Cassiopeia are always visible in the northern night sky whatever the time of year.*

Astronomers divide the sky into eighty-eight constellations. If you wanted to see all of them you would have to live on the equator, where both northern and southern stars can be seen. An alternative is to move about Earth changing your observing position as you go. Each time you travel, use the chance to explore the changing sky above. All observers will find the southern sky very rich in star fields. The centre of our Galaxy lies in the direction of Sagittarius, the constellation that marks the southerly point of the Sun's path. Further south is the smallest constellation in the whole sky, Crux (below). It may be the smallest but it is easy to identify. Its brilliant stars stand out against the background of the Milky Way. Close by are the dark, Coal Sack nebula, and the Jewel Box, one of the finest of star clusters. Use Crux as a stepping stone to other stars. At either side are the constellations of Centaurus and Carina.

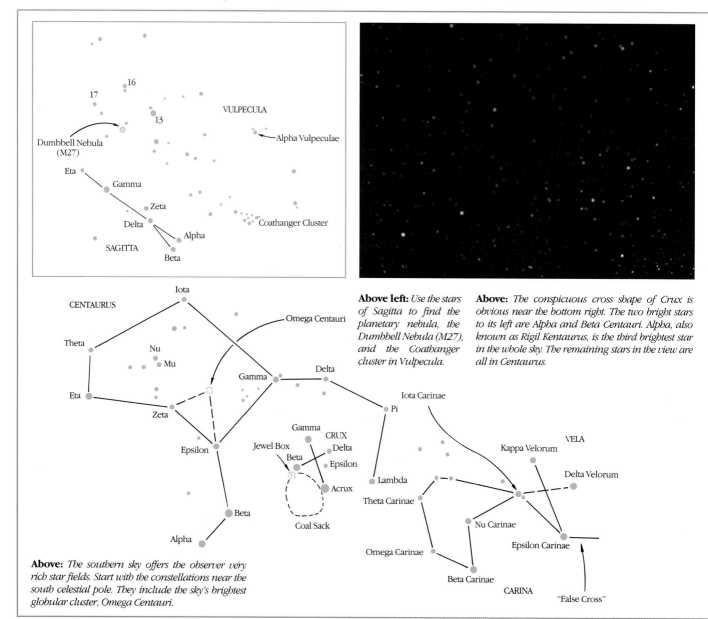

Above left: *Use the stars of Sagitta to find the planetary nebula, the Dumbbell Nebula (M27), and the Coathanger cluster in Vulpecula.*

Above: *The conspicuous cross shape of Crux is obvious near the bottom right. The two bright stars to its left are Alpha and Beta Centauri. Alpha, also known as Rigil Kentaurus, is the third brightest star in the whole sky. The remaining stars in the view are all in Centaurus.*

Above: *The southern sky offers the observer very rich star fields. Start with the constellations near the south celestial pole. They include the sky's brightest globular cluster, Omega Centauri.*

A sight that can be shared by northern and southern observers is the Summer Triangle. Three bright stars in different constellations make a prominent triangle in the sky. They are Deneb in Cygnus, Vega in Lyra and Altair in Aquila (below right). They can be seen overhead by northern observers in the summer months, hence their name. At the same time southern observers see them in the centre of their northerly sky. The individual constellations are also worth looking at. Deneb and other bright stars form the outline of Cygnus, the swan. The swan's head, Albireo, is seen to be two stars when viewed through binoculars. Epsilon Lyrae is a well known double double star. Nearby is the Ring Nebula, M57. Regular observations will show Eta Aquilae is a variable star, changing brightness in a little over seven days. Once you have mastered these objects use the information in the rest of this book to decide where to look next.

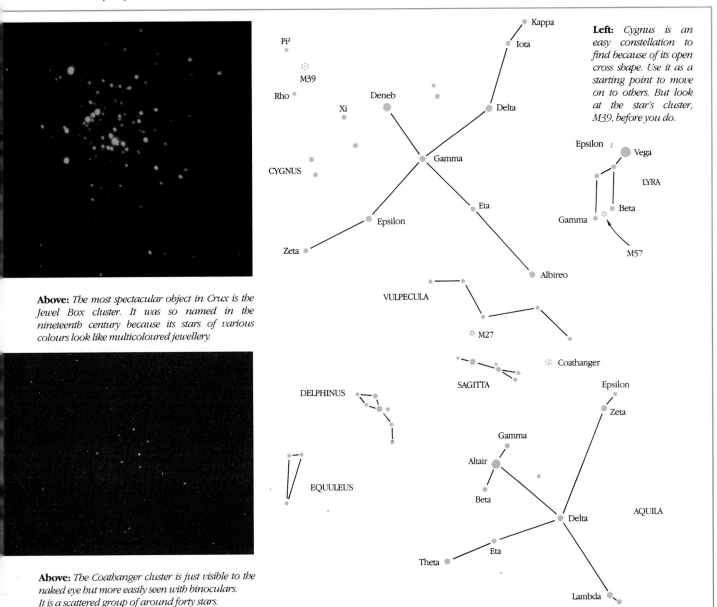

Above: *The most spectacular object in Crux is the Jewel Box cluster. It was so named in the nineteenth century because its stars of various colours look like multicoloured jewellery.*

Above: *The Coathanger cluster is just visible to the naked eye but more easily seen with binoculars. It is a scattered group of around forty stars.*

Left: *Cygnus is an easy constellation to find because of its open cross shape. Use it as a starting point to move on to others. But look at the star's cluster, M39, before you do.*

GLOSSARY

A

Absolute Magnitude The apparent magnitude a star would have if it were to be viewed from a distance of 10 Parsecs (32·6 light years)

Aphelion The point in its orbit around the Sun at which an object is furthest from the Sun

Apogee The point in its orbit around the Earth at which an object is furthest from the Earth

Apparent Magnitude The apparent visual brightness of a star or other celestial object

Ashen Light A dim glow sometimes seen on the dark side of Venus when it is visible as a thin crescent. The cause is not fully understood

Asteroid Another name for MINOR PLANET

Aurora Glow seen over the polar regions which occurs when energised particles from the Sun react with particles in the Earth's upper atmosphere

Autumnal Equinox The point at which the apparent path of the Sun, moving from north to south, crosses the celestial equator

B

Binary Star A system of two stars orbiting each other around their common centre of gravity

Black Hole A region of space around a very small and extremely massive collapsed star within which the gravitational field is so intense that not even light can escape

Celestial Equator A projection of the Earth's equator onto the celestial sphere, equidistant from the celestial poles and dividing the celestial sphere into two hemispheres

Celestial Poles The points on the celestial sphere directly above the north and south terrestrial poles around which the celestial sphere appears to rotate

Celestial Sphere The imaginary sphere of stars surrounding the Earth

Comet An object comprised of a mixture of gas, dust and ice and which travels around the Sun in an orbit that is usually very eccentric

Constellation One of a total of 88 arbitary groupings of stars on the celestial sphere

D

Double Star Two stars which appear to be close to each other in the sky. Binary stars are physically related while optical doubles simply lie in the same line of sight as seen from Earth

E

Eclipse The obscuration of one celestial object by another, such as the Sun by the Moon during a solar eclipse

Ecliptic The apparent path of the Sun through the sky. The ecliptic passes through a band of constellations called the Zodiac

Equinox The autumnal and vernal equinoxes are the two points at which the ecliptic crosses the celestial equator

F

Fireball A very bright meteor or shooting star

G

Galactic Cluster Another name for an open cluster

Galaxy A vast collection of stars, gas and dust measuring many light years across

Globular Cluster Large, almost spherical collections of old stars

H

Hubble Classification A system, devised by Edwin Hubble, in which Galaxies are classified according to their shape

L

Light Year The distance which a ray of light would travel in a year, equal to approximately 6,000,000,000,000 miles (10,000,000,000,000km). This is a standard unit of length used by astronomers

Local Group A cluster of Galaxies of which our own is a member

M

Magnitude See Absolute Magnitude and Apparent Magnitude

Meteor A streak of light in the sky seen as the result of the destruction through atmospheric friction of a meteoroid in the Earth's atmosphere

Meteorite A meteoroid which is sufficiently large to at least partially survive the fall through Earth's atmosphere

Meteoroid A term applied to particles of interplanetary meteoritic debris

Milky Way The faint band of light crossing the sky which is the result of the combined light from the thousands of stars that lie along the main plane of our Galaxy

Minor Planet One of the large number of small planetary bodies which orbit the Sun largely between the orbits of Mars and Jupiter

Moon The Earth's only natural satellite

N

Nebula An interstellar cloud of gas and dust

Neutron Star The remnant of a massive star which has exploded as a supernova

Nova A Star which suddenly flares up to perhaps many times its original brightness before fading again

O

Occultation The temporary covering up of one celestial object, such as a star, by another, such as the Moon

Open Cluster A loose and irregular shaped collection of stars

Opposition The point in its orbit at which a superior planet is directly opposite the Sun in the sky

Orbit The closed path of one object around another

P

Parallax The apparent shift of a nearby object against a more distant background when viewed from two points

Parsec The distance at which a star would have a parallax of one second of arc. equal to 3·26 light years

Penumbra The lighter part of a sunspot. Also the area of partial shadow around the main cone of shadow cast by the Moon during a solar eclipse or Earth during a lunar eclipse

Perigee The point in its orbit around the Earth at which an object is closest to the Earth

Perihelion The point in its orbit around the Sun at which an object is closest to the Sun

Planet One of the nine major members of the Sun's family

Prime Meridian The meridian that passes through the vernal equinox

Pulsar A rapidly-spinning neutron star which gives off regular bursts of radiation

Q

Quasar Extremely remote and highly luminous objects, now believed to be the cores of active Galaxies

S

Satellite A small object orbiting a larger one

Solar System The collective description given to the system dominated by the Sun and including the planets, minor planets, comets, planetary satellites and interplanetary debris that travel in orbits around the Sun

Solar Wind The constant stream of energised particles emitted by the Sun

Solstice The positions in the sky at which the Sun is at its maximum angular distance (declination) from the celestial equator

Supernova A huge stellar explosion involving the destruction of a massive star and resulting in a sudden brightening

Synodic Period The interval between successive oppositions of a planet or other object in the Solar System

U

Umbra The darker part of a sunspot. Also the main cone of shadow cast by the Moon during a solar eclipse or the Earth during a lunar eclipse

V

Variable Star Stars whose brightness varies, these effects being due either to changes taking place within the star itself or the periodic obscuration of one member of a binary star by another. These systems are called eclipsing binaries

Vernal Equinox The point at which the apparent path of the Sun, moving from south to north, crosses the celestial equator

Z

Zenith The point in the sky directly above the observer

Page references set in *italic* type refer to subjects mentioned in illustration captions.

Picture credits